The Choral Director's Guid

The Choral Director's Guide to Sanity ...and Success!

How to Develop a Flourishing Middle School/Junior High School Choral Program

Randy Pagel with Linda Spevacek

Heritage Music Press
A DIVISION OF THE LORENZ CORPORATION
Box 802 / Dayton, OH 45401-0802

Editor: Kris Kropff
Type Design: Digital Dynamite, Inc.
Cover Design: Nancy Chifala

Heritage Music Press
A division of The Lorenz Corporation
P.O. Box 802
Dayton, OH 45401-0802
www.lorenz.com

Printed in the United States of America

ISBN: 0-89328-172-7

"Only A Teacher" is used by kind permission of Dr. Ivan Fitzwater, Professor Emeritus of Education, Trinity University.

Contents

Contents (continued)

Editor's Preface

Beginning from a basic outline of topics and writing toward a common goal, Randy Pagel and Linda Spevacek went to work, each contributing specifically to those areas of their particular expertise. Rather than merging their insights into a single voice, we've arranged *The Choral Director's Guide to Sanity...and Success!* in a way that preserves the unique voice of each author.

To this end, you'll note that some chapters are written by a single author while others include the contributions of both authors. In the case of the latter, the contributions may exist as two parts of a single chapter or in the form of commentary by Linda Spevacek, highlighted as "From my perspective..." Only those chapters written by Linda Spevacek are credited. All other material was written by Randy Pagel. A listing of the contributions of each is provided below.

Randy Pagel—Chapters 1-8; Chapter 9, Part 1; Chapter 10; Chapter 11, Part 2; Chapter 12, Part 1; Chapters 13-16; and Chapters 18-19.

Linda Spevacek—Chapter 9, Part 2; Chapter 11, Part 1; Chapter 12, Part 2; Chapter 17 and Chapters 20-21. The "From my perspective..." commentaries appear in Chapters 10, 15 and 18.

Who knows which way the wind will blow in each of our lives? Who knows who will touch our lives in ways that we can only imagine?

Our sincere heartfelt thanks go to the many teachers in our lives that have molded and encouraged our love of music and teaching. This is our gift to them, and to you, as we give back to the present and future generations of teachers some of what we've been given by so many teachers who have inspired us along our own journeys. We hope this book provides encouragement, insight, new information, and helpful tips for you and your students for many years to come.

The number of people to thank goes back many years for both of us. To our many teachers along the way—the teachers that have encouraged, commented and made suggestions—thank you. Our special thanks go to Mary Lynn Lightfoot, our editor at Heritage Music Press, Larry Pugh, President of the Publishing Divisions of The Lorenz Corporation, Kris Kropff, who edited this book, and of course, Geoff Lorenz, CEO of the Lorenz Corporation, who makes it all possible.

Introduction

You have spent many years since your childhood involved with school activities, learning from teachers, enjoying time with fellow students, and learning many exciting things in the classroom. You dedicated hours upon hours and years upon years developing your reading, writing, mathematic, scientific, and social skills. You have enjoyed being involved in many scholastic, extra-curricular and team sport activities both at school and throughout the community. You have experienced a great deal of success in some of these endeavors you have been involved in, but even beyond that, you spent many years practicing and developing your skills taking private lessons on a musical instrument. After all of this, you reach the end of your senior year of high school and it's now time to decide on a career. You have chosen to be a choral educator. In fact, there is no other occupation that you can even think of doing because your life has been so fulfilled with the camaraderie of your classmates, the activities you were involved with, and the many lifetime experiences you had, including being involved with musicals and traveling with your chorus to sing. You want nothing more than to pass on this wonderful experience to the next generation of students and beyond, so you enter college as a music education major; your goal is to be a choral director.

During college you take a veritable string of classes on professional education, including the psychology of children, giving proper evaluations, dealing with exceptional children, and the legalese of working as a teacher. You took method classes in music and learned how to conduct music in proper patterns. All along, you were involved in several activities and sang in the chorus. Finally it was time to begin your student teaching. Although it may not have been exactly what you expected, all in all, it was a rather rewarding experience. Alas, you received your degree, and after many tense moments, you finally got what you always wanted—a job teaching chorus, and more specifically, it was a job which includes teaching middle school!

Teaching middle school students can be the most incredibly rewarding, uplifting and worthwhile experience for any person. On the flip side, teaching middle school can also be the most incredibly painful, exhausting and useless experience for a teacher. In order to get the best of this paradox, you must be armed and ready with as much knowledge and experience as possible. This includes learning from those already in the field, as well as learning from and building on your own personal experiences.

Middle school students are in the stage of their lives where they can experience the greatest achievements, make the greatest strides, and build and cherish memories for a lifetime. Middle school students are also in the stage of their life where they can experience the greatest disasters, make horrible decisions affecting their entire life, and have memories they would just as soon forget. In order for middle school students to get the best of this paradox, you must be armed and ready with your own knowledge and experience and continue learning from other teachers and people in the middle school field to help you work with and guide middle school students effectively. In both cases, it's up to *you*—the teacher—to prepare yourself for your own teaching and for your students' educational experience and social development.

Indeed, the middle school student is reaching perhaps the most important fork in the road in the journey of life. Going down one road can lead to disaster, yet going down the other road can lead to unabated success. As the middle school teacher, you may be the one and only person who has the trust and influence to direct a student down the right path. It's up to any teacher to accept this great responsibility and to prepare accordingly.

PART ONE

A Music Teacher is a Teacher

Managing Your Classroom for Sanity...and Success!

It's the first day of school; perhaps your first day of teaching! The students come in quietly, find a place to sit, and are not quite sure what to expect; perhaps they do not know many of the students around them, so they remain quiet until you have spoken. As you hand out classroom rules and explain your expectations, you feel yourself getting a little nervous. You start rambling on about yourself, about how involved you've been in education over the years and how you've always wanted to be a teacher. Pretty soon, the students are getting a little twitchy, and you feel yourself beginning to sweat. Your body language says you're not sure quite what to expect, frankly, because you are not even quite sure of yourself. In those few seconds of dead time, a restless student pokes another to get his attention, and suddenly, the class begins to focus on that distraction.

You aren't quite sure what you said or did to cause this situation, but now it seems as though the entire class is unraveling. At this moment, everything that was on your mind to tell the class over the remaining 45 minutes has escaped your head and panic sets in. It occurs to you that everything you ever learned in college (not to mention your thirteen years of prior schooling) never prepared you for what to do next. Finally, you hear a voice inside your head saying, "Why did you ever decide to be a teacher?"

It doesn't matter how great your musical skills are, how much you love children, how many conducting awards you won in college, or even what a genuinely good person you are if you don't have the most important tool for any teacher in any field—classroom management. This tool is essential if we are to get any of our educational philosophies across to our students, build any trust between ourselves and our students, or even begin to compete with the many outside influences that creep into our classroom.

Even though we would like for each and every one of our students to come to class well-mannered, well-dressed, well-kept, and fully prepared—physically, emotionally, and educationally—this will never happen. We have no control over our students' home environments. We have very little control over how our current students have been educated by their elementary teachers or if they have attained the skill level required to attend middle school.

But teachers do have a great deal of control, indeed an enormous amount of control, over what goes on inside their classrooms once the students arrive. Regardless of any excess baggage outside your room, the students will quickly adjust to your classroom climate—a climate set by you, the teacher. The amount that the students learn is based on the effectiveness of the teacher. An effective teacher is truly an effective leader. The President of the United States sets the tone for the country, the governor for the state, the manager for the store, the principal for the school, and the teacher for the classroom. The only way for students to gain achievement is through the leadership of the teacher, *not the other way around*. The same is true for other leaders. If any leader is unsure of his or her leadership, or is constantly changing direction with the wind, everything will eventually get out of control. This is especially true in the classroom.

Regardless of the background of your students, the amount of money poured (or dripped) into the school system, or the support of the community, it's *your* classroom. These are *your* students, under *your* direction. The effective teacher teaches the students how to behave properly, and accepts the responsibility of each student's educational outcome. It's up to the teachers to prepare themselves, set the stage, and dedicate themselves to teaching their students *until they learn*. Anything less than a total commitment is unacceptable! Once these elements are in place, the students *will* respond to the teaching in the classroom rather quickly—it's up to the teacher to make the first move!

The teacher's classroom structure and organization in a classroom is the most important factor for increasing student achievement. Before any teaching strategies can be exercised, the room should be organized in a way that allows anyone walking in—students included—to immediately see that you are enthusiastic about your job, organized, efficient, and student-friendly. Your classroom's appearance is the first impression your students experience—give them a great one.

Once you are mentally prepared, have set the stage with an organized-looking classroom, and are ready to give a total commitment, it's time to put into motion your teaching ideas and strategies. The classroom management tools presented here are not intended to be the end-all of classroom management. Rather, its intention is to give you ideas and hints to think about when you are teaching. Each and every teacher is different, and each and every student is different. It's up to you to take your personality, along with the dynamics of your students, and glean the management tools to best work with your situation.

We tend to get what we expect.

—N. V. Peale

Despite your best teaching efforts, there is a good chance that you will receive nothing more from your students than your lowest expectations. If you allow thoughts like, "kids in middle school can't focus for more than 5 minutes" or "this is as much as I can ask from *this* group" to creep into your mind while teaching, you do a disservice to yourself and your students. Before the first student enters your classroom, set your expectations high. Expect the best from yourself, and expect the best from your students.

If you expect the students to behave properly and achieve at a high level, regardless of their background, there is an excellent chance that you will receive at least as much as you expect, if not more! Why? Because your body language will reflect this attitude; your voice and speech pattern will become more positive. Students will immediately pick up on these qualities and mirror your energy. You become more uplifted, and your mind becomes better focused on what you actually want to teach instead of constantly dealing with classroom disruptions. It's a win-win situation!

Example is not the main thing influencing others, it is the only thing.

—Albert Schweitzer

The students are a reflection of the teacher, plain and simple. If you are enthusiastic about your job, your students will be enthusiastic about their learning. If your appearance and demeanor are professional, the students (and your colleagues) will treat you as a professional. If your room is neat and clean, the students will see that you take pride in your classroom and, in turn, will take pride in your class. If you carry yourself with confidence, the students will carry themselves with confidence. If you are fair and honest, your students will be fair and honest.

Once you have led by setting an excellent example, you can now help your students do the same for others. In every appropriate situation, find a way to convince your students that they should set a good example for others to follow. This can be most effective with a student who has great leadership skills, who may otherwise use these skills to constantly interrupt your class. Try a simple, private talk with the student: "You have terrific leadership skills because you have a talent to get others to follow you. You could use this to your advantage and make this class even better if you would use your leadership skills in a positive way. I would like to see you lead by example in a positive way." When students are given the tools to lead by example, everyone, especially you, wins.

Failure to prepare is preparing to fail.

John Woodon

It's up to you—and only you—to fully prepare yourself to teach effectively and to meet or exceed your own expectations and those of your students. You must fully develop your lessons and have a variety of ways to teach these lessons to get the best out of your students. This includes always over-preparing your lessons and having many activities planned in case there are a few minutes remaining in the class period. If you have only one lesson planned for the class period and things don't go the way you intended, you will lose the attention and respect of your students.

There's an old saying that idleness is the devil's playground. This is especially true with middle school students. They are like bloodhounds when it comes to sensing teachers who are running out of things to do. If you have nothing else prepared for them, they *will* have things prepared for you!

Have only a few rules, but expect each of them to be followed.

Students, as with people in general, will have a tendency to follow a rule or two if they feel it's fair, necessary and in their best interest. But if you have a lengthy list of behavior expectations for your students, along with an equally lengthy list of progressive consequences, you will quickly lose the attention of your students. Decide which one, two or perhaps three rules are the most necessary to enable you to teach effectively, and for the students to learn effectively. One may be to respect others. Although only one rule is listed, be prepared to discuss with the students what respecting others actually means: stop talking when the teacher is giving instructions; keep your hands to yourselves; try your best. Once the student has examples of respecting others, including you, an improper behavior can be corrected by a simple statement such as, "Is that respecting others?" With this statement, the actual behavior of flicking another student's ear, for example, is not verbally reinforced to the student or the class.

An important caveat to this approach: students will not respect you until you first respect them. It's never appropriate to ask a student to respect you. You have to earn it. Students, especially at the middle school level, *want* to have people to look up to and to respect, regardless of what they may show on the outside. Give them this opportunity by giving them your respect. The rewards down the road will be great.

Other rules can be put in place simply by effective classroom management. Take "Be in your seat when the bell rings" as an example. Without even writing down the rule, it may be automatically followed by your students if you begin the class on time, and with a quick, energetic activity which immediately gets all students involved with undivided attention. The students will quickly learn that because the teacher begins on time, they must arrive on time. Also, if an enthusiastic, worthwhile activity begins the class, the students will want to arrive on time and check it out.

Such activities may include a "quote of the day" or "word of the day" which the students are to discuss, or even write down. You may begin a vocal exercise as the students are walking in (even before the bell rings). You may stand at the door giving each student a high-five as they enter. Whatever it may be, it's human nature to want to be a part of the action. If the action is in your class, the students will want to be there. If it's not, they will want to remain where the action was before they came to your class, or worse yet, create their own action at the expense of your class time.

Oftentimes, a list of consequences, usually progressive in nature, immediately follows the presentation of the rules. Such a list may signal to students that the rules have been broken before, even five or more times by the same student! Also, progressive discipline typically includes a phone call home or a trip to the principal. Although this may be necessary at times, it shows that you are no longer in control of the situation and must pass it along to someone else. Talk about losing respect!

Further, it's always important to talk *with* the student if something goes wrong, and in private if at all possible. Another sure way to lose the respect of your students is to embarrass or humiliate them in front of their peers. This doesn't mean that an improper behavior cannot be immediately corrected in the classroom, but it doesn't have to become the center of attention. If you talk with the offending student in private and explain why his or her behavior was inappropriate, you will be respected for the dignity you helped the student keep, and there will be a much greater chance that your rules will be followed in the future.

Well begun is half done.

—Aristotle

Why does every major league baseball stadium sell out on Opening Day year after year? Because it's the most optimistic day of the baseball season. Every team, including the one you follow, is tied for first place. Luckily, on the first day of school, the students have this same optimism. They always come in quietly, waiting to learn what is expected from them. This is the only day of the year when this will happen. Capitalize on it! The presentation you give to your students on the first day of the year will set the stage for the rest of the year. Perhaps a simple, "I like the way everyone came in this morning on time and took their places quietly. I will expect this every day," would be a great way to set the stage for your opening-day presentation.

All day long, students are going to hear the same thing from each and every teacher: the 15 rules to be followed; the 5 progressive consequences; and the boring stories used by the teacher to fill the dead time. Be different. Get their attention right away. Get them up and singing! Send a signal that you love what you do. The students will react in turn.

Another opening-day perk—for the most part, the students arrive with all of their school supplies, their new school clothes, zero outstanding homework assignments, and an excitement about seeing friends they have not seen all summer. They are actually glad to be relieved of the boredom which set in somewhere in late July, early August. Like you, they are armed and ready to go with loads of enthusiasm and high expectations.

The first day is the time to seek out a student who looks anxious or rambunctious and greet him with a simple, "Those are some snazzy shoes you have one!" A simple act like this may just make the student's whole day. You've also established an important, positive connection that this student will remember. Establishing that connection with every student is important, but there is always a chance that this student you lifted up was the one who had previously decided you were the teacher he was going to create trouble for. Because of this one small thing you said to this particular student, you may have saved yourself several incidents of grief that may have happened throughout the year.

Now is the time to get things done, and fast. Give your expectations, take attendance and get those students up and singing! Here's a great plan for the first minute of day one:

1. Have the students say "Zing." They will probably be shy about it because it's the first day, so you say, "We need to have more energy than that! Say *Zing*." Now they say it with energy, so you reinforce with enthusiasm, "That sounds great!"

2. Have the students sing—in unison F major for SATB or A major (below middle C) for boys' unchanged voices—"Zing, Zing, Zing, Zing, Zing" [1, 2, 3, 2, 1]. Work up and down. Do not over stretch the first day. You want the students to feel totally successful on day one.

3. Now "Zing, Zing, Zing, Zing, Zing, Zah, Zah, Zah, Zah" [1, 2, 3, 4, 5, 4, 3, 2, 1].

4. Have students do this individually. If this is done with enthusiasm the first day, they will not be shy about singing in front of each other, especially if you 1) pick a few students who you see and hear will do a great job and 2) do not make a big deal about singing alone. Instead of being shy, they will want to take a turn singing, most even raising their hand to volunteer!

5. Have the students learn an entire song, either in unison or a round. Make sure they experience success the first day with their choral singing.

You did it! You got them to do something the first day that they didn't do in their other classes! They stood up and sang, and at a great level of success. Most even sang once by themselves! This success will be built upon day after day because the foundation has been set on day one!

Students will not care how much you know until they know how much you care.

—Proverb

The easiest way to show the students that you care—and consequently one of the best classroom management tools—is to learn the students' names as quickly as possible. When taking attendance on the first day, learn and memorize a few students' names. Then, sometime during the first day of class, use those names nonchalantly during a discussion. You will inevitably hear a student say, "He already knows all of our names!" Of course you may not know everyone's name yet, but the students who are sitting in your classroom feel as though you are their own personal teacher.

Play a game to learn the students' names: have the students stand and form a circle. Choose a starting point and ask the first ten or fifteen students to tell you their names. Pick any student in that group, point and say his or her name. The students may sit once their name has been given correctly. Repeat until you've gotten through the circle. (Although this can take an entire class period, be sure to leave about ten minutes for singing, building on what you did yesterday.) The next day, ask the students to return to the same place in the circle and repeat, this time without being given their names. If you are feeling confident, ask the students to mix up the circle. Finally, ask the students to go back to the risers and have them all stand. When you point to them, you say their name and they sit. Do this until all of the names are learned. This activity usually takes three days or fewer, with less than half the class time used the second day and only five or ten minutes used the third day.

Have a student take a turn identifying the students one by one as well. Getting students involved in this way will excite the class. It will also keep students attentive as they silently play along with each other in preparation for their turn. Mostly, though, it shows that you are a cooperative teacher and you are open to the students having some say and input in the class.

I know, you're thinking you cannot possibly take this much time to just learn the students' names. But you are not just learning their names; you are building class camaraderie. You are getting the students enthused about your class and your classroom environment. You are showing the students that you care about them individually. Throughout the school year, you can really show the students how much you care by using their names in the hallway in front of their peers when you just say "Hi!" Once again, this seemingly irrelevant gesture will strengthen the connection the students feel for you and they will automatically behave better in your class. Further, if a behavior situation arises, the students will be more open to correcting the problem when you talk with them privately simply because you called them by name outside of your classroom. Indeed, you cannot possibly *not* take the time to learn their names!

The time to repair the roof is when the sun is shining.

—John F. Kennedy

In a typical classroom, the teacher disciplines when the problem occurs. You must think differently! Even though the sun is shining now, take every appropriate opportunity you can to repair the roof, because one day it will be raining. If you have the students' attention and respect within the first week, it's much easier to deal with the small problems that will inevitably occur by the end of the first week. Calmly deal with small problems, coaching the students to understand why they should behave properly.

One common problem is two students whispering or talking during your lesson. You certainly did not give permission for the students to talk while you are teaching and you didn't encourage this kind of behavior by allowing for any dead time. It's simply the students testing the waters. If they are able to chatter without being noticed or acknowledged, the entire class will get the signal that this behavior is acceptable in your classroom. Instead, when the chatter first occurs give both of the students a look as if to say, "stop it, *now*." Do not get excited or overly verbal when the problem first occurs.

Another powerful weapon to disarm student chattering is to simply move into their territory, which includes standing over them. All along, you never miss a beat in your lesson or change your speaking voice. Most of the time the students will get the message to stop talking. You can also diffuse problem behavior before it starts by getting out from behind the piano. It's easy for choral educators to plant themselves behind the piano and stay there the entire hour, but you need to use any opportunity to move about. Don't become predictable; keep students guessing. Otherwise, your constant position will become a signal for the students to chatter.

If it should happen that the students do not stop talking even though you gave them a look or moved into their territory, it's time to quickly explain to the class why this is not acceptable. A simple, "When you are talking while I am teaching, it becomes more difficult for you to learn. I do not want you to not understand something simply because you were talking while I was teaching." The use of the word "you" doesn't directly attack the talking students in front of the class and it's a means of prevention. Each student hears the word "you" and gets the message, not just the talking students. If you handle this in a calm and collected manner, the talking students will usually stop, and you have gained their respect because you took care of the problem without raising your voice and without losing your cool. Also, you did not single out any student. All of the students will respect this, and they will remember it, helping to nip a lot of future problems in the bud.

Silence is the best weapon of power.

—Charles de Gaulle

There will come a day when the students decide to walk in at will and talk up a storm. It's as if they all called each other the night before and decided to make your class a zoo the next morning. You would be willing to give half of your salary for a remote control with a mute button—even more for one that includes a pause button. Who knows why these days happen, but they do and it's up to you to correct this situation before it gets out of hand, becomes a habit for the students, and eventually an acceptable behavior. This is definitely a time for you to be at your best, which in this instance means stand patiently, not looking bothered or flustered, and wait for the class to get quiet on their own.

Ongoing misbehavior is a silent plea for a teacher to take charge, but be careful when taking charge. Wisdom from Thomas Jefferson says that if you are angry, count to ten before saying anything; if you are really angry, count to one hundred. It has also been shown that when dealing with adolescents the best way to calm them down is to act as if their behavior doesn't bother you. Fight the temptation to blow up and yell and scream at the students because of the noise. Instead, stand in front of the class, almost like a statue. You may be surprised how quickly the students get quiet on their own. It usually takes 30-45 seconds or less. Another win-win situation: the students did not see you lose your cool, and even more importantly, it was *their* decision to stop talking. That is powerful.

The best way to win an argument is to avoid it.

—Dale Carnegie

The worst thing a teacher can do is feed an argument started by a student who thinks he know everything, but who will eventually need to save face in front of his peers if confronted. A leading question like, "Why do we have to stand up when we sing?" is all it takes to start such a situation, which can quickly escalate if not handled properly. Know that this question isn't meant to elicit an answer. Rather, this student wants to see if you need to explain yourself or your teaching methods. He also wants to see how corny your answers will be, or how flustered you will become. Or maybe the student is hoping you will give in to his question and have the students sit down, at which point he wins and you lose.

Any such disruption can be avoided by simply and calmly replying to the student, "Why *do* we have to stand up when we sing?" The majority of the time, the student will not say anything back, but will get the message loud and clear: answer the question yourself, for now, and see me after class if it's still that important to you. You said "this is not the time for an interruption" without saying it and stopped the argument in its tracks.

There are many situations when a question is best answered with the exact same question. Use this approach to your advantage to avoid an argument or conflict with a student, and to keep your class from escalating out of control.

You may have to fight a battle more than once to win it.

—Margaret Thatcher

Students who do not get the answer they were searching for will often ask the same question with a different inflection, or with different words altogether. If you made a decision when answering a question the first time—and you feel it was the right one—you should come back with the same answer with the same inflection and in the same tone of voice. If you add a simple, "I understand where you are coming from, but..." before the repeated answer, you validate what the students have to say, but you stick to your guns. You gave the answer you felt was best for the students and the situation. The students may be upset with you or your answer, but in the long run you will gain their respect and they will admire your courage and ability to stick with your decision. They will also understand that as individuals and as a class they will be the beneficiary of your validation and decisiveness later.

The greatest lesson in life is to know that even fools are right sometimes.

—Winston Churchill

Some of the greatest things you can learn come from people who seem to have no idea what they are doing, but bring a fresh, new perspective to the situation. (Think about the bus stuck in a tunnel—engineer after engineer came along with complex solutions but it was a kid who suggested taking the air out of the tires.) If you are seeking advice after a chorus concert or performance, always ask a non-musician in the crowd. Chances are, these casual non-musicians will represent the largest segment of your audience. Why wouldn't you want their input?

The same is true for students. Although they don't have the same formal education you have nor the experience you have as a teacher, they may know a thing or two about what is best. Whether it's bringing more pizzazz to a performance or making your class more enjoyable for the students to attend, allow your students to offer their input.

Because student input so often comes in the form of a question, it's important for all educators to embrace the philosophy that there is no such thing as a stupid question. A cliché, yes, but one that is worth emphasizing. The "stupid" question may be asked by a student who gathered all of his courage just to be able to raise his hand. And while it may be a stupid question to you, it's not to him. Even if his question is "way out there," a respectful answer may open the door to future questions and contributions.

Do the class, as well as yourself, a favor by allowing the students the latitude to ask any question in an unabated manner. Just because the question or statement doesn't necessarily agree with your viewpoint, do not snuff out the student. Rather, say something like, "I never really thought of it that way," or "That's a different way of thinking—good for you!" In addition to keeping the lesson moving, a response like this validates the students and shows the class that you have respect for their viewpoint, even if it doesn't necessarily agree with your own. It also encourages all students to think on their own, and, in turn, learn at a higher level.

Being defeated is often a temporary condition. Giving up is what makes it permanent.

—Marilyn von Savant

There are several times throughout the school year when you feel as though your class has knocked you silly and you are down for the count. When you are dealing with many students, i.e. a large chorus class, unexpected and unpleasant things *are* going to happen. It's up to you as the teacher to figure out what went wrong and what you can, and will, do to fix the problem.

If you said something that you feel badly about, apologize to the class. They will respect you for it. If you handled a situation in a way you knew didn't work or even escalated the situation, talk with the other party, be it another teacher, a business person, or even a student from the class, about what you could have done differently to make the situation better.

Although many people look up to you, everyone—including your students—understands that you are human and not immune to mistakes. Tomorrow is a new day for everyone. Take advantage of that while you are finding solutions to fix the problems of today.

It must be peace without victory...Only a peace between equals can last.

—Woodrow Wilson

Do you know any teachers who blame the principal or other teachers or parents or even society for the problems of their students? Teachers who wish all of their students could read music at a high level? Teachers who get frustrated with other teachers who don't think that music is important? While it's easy to fall into this trap, as choral educators we really don't have time for it. Thankfully, we have a choice. Instead of reacting to a storm in the class with blaming, criticizing or even giving up, keep the peace in your room by reinforcing the behaviors you want, both with your words and your actions.

We teach our students how to maintain the peace amongst themselves by not simply establishing rules, but by always practicing and reminding the students of these rules. This must be done on their level and sometimes on their terms. If the students are behaving just because the big bad teacher tells them to, they will be less inclined to follow the rules. But if the students are reminded of the rules and they agree with why the rules should be followed, they will definitely follow the rules more consistently. Every attempt should be made to give the students the feeling that this is their classroom; that the behaviors you expect of them are also behaviors they should expect of themselves.

Winning is a habit, unfortunately, so is losing.

—Vince Lombardi

When a team is winning, everything seems to be falling into place and clicking on all cylinders. Everyone on the team is happy. When a team is losing, the opposite seems to happen, and strategies used to "fix it" seem to make it worse. Instead of saying, "We have to stop dropping the ball," what would happen if we said, "We were winning more when we focused on securing the ball"? This same strategy can be used in your classroom.

You have a finite pool of attention to give to individual students clamoring for it and an entire class that requires it. Do not waste this valuable attention by reinforcing negative behavior. It's a lose-lose situation. It will grind your spirit down to nothing, but worse yet, the students will soon learn that the only attention they can receive is for negative behavior—a sure way to drive otherwise well-behaved students to misbehave.

When you see a student doing something positive, verbally reinforce it by calling attention to the positive behavior. Not only will the student feel good about being praised in front of her peers and respond better to your teaching, the other students will be aurally reinforced with the positive praise or the positive behavior and will strive to achieve the positive behavior in the future.

By turning "Stop slouching" into "Great posture!" you create a win-win situation. It's up to you to respond in the best way.

Do not measure yourself by what you have accomplished, but by what you should have accomplished with your ability.

—John Wooden

A pervading theory of education is to teach to the average ability of the class. The logic being that the less-than-average students will elevate to match the average, the average students (considered to be the majority) will catch on easily to what they are supposed to learn, and the above-average students will thrive no matter what. Why embrace this kind of defeatist attitude before you even enter the classroom? Why underestimate your students? When the students catch on to this mediocrity, how much respect will they have left for you?

There may be others who will say that teaching to the top will do more harm than good. These are the same type of people who feel that a piece of music is too hard for the given age level of students, or that the students are too young to handle adversity. Always remember that we are there to educate our students. There are times when you select a piece of music or teach a lesson and know that all of your students will catch on quickly and feel successful. Hopefully, this success will be a catalyst to bigger and better things. If you challenge the students to reach a higher level, they may not do as well now as they will some time later, but at least you exposed them to a higher level of thinking, and you gave them something to perhaps explore later when they are older and wiser. Always remember that without *risk* there is no *art*. Even beyond that, if you risk nothing, then you risk everything.

When you lose a game, everyone remembers what went wrong. Accordingly, you will definitely remember the correct answer to a test question you got wrong. If you came close in a spelling bee, you will never forget how to spell the word that eliminated you. So remember that when you are teaching, teach to the top and all others will rise, even when the others appear to not catch on at first.

If you can't convince them, confuse them.

—Harry S Truman

Just as we have nine months in a school year to teach our students successfully, baseball players have nine innings in a game in which to win. A "flame thrower" pitching in the consistent mid-90s and blowing the ball past the batters will get strike after strike for the first few innings. As the game goes on, though, the hitters adjust to the timing of the previously invincible pitcher and hit the ball successfully. This is when successful pitchers reach into their bag of tricks and throw a "change up." Teachers must do the same thing. Do things differently often—get off autopilot.

You can have the most successful method of teaching under the sun, but it will become ineffective if you become complacent. Students change year to year, week to week, even day to day (especially in middle school) and you must adjust. Be willing to try new strategies or abandon those that are no longer effective. Never fall into the automatic-pilot, going-through-the-motions trap. It's up to you to change with the times, and keep yourself, as well as your students, on the cutting edge at all times.

Take different tempos even if they don't necessarily go with the style of the music. Instead of burying yourself behind the piano, get out in front of the choir. Better yet, stand with the choir and build camaraderie! Move your arms more when you teach, walk around the room when you are speaking, make eye contact with as many students as possible, and engage your students in the conversation. As long as it goes with the flow of your personality, do the unexpected, no matter what it is. Unpredictability will become your best asset. And as Harry S Truman says, "If you can't convince them, confuse them." It may just work!

Idleness and pride tax with a heavier hand than kings and parliaments.

—Benjamin Franklin

The saying, "Me, me, me is dull, dull, dull," is just as true when teaching a class as it is when conversing with friends. Although the enthusiasm that you have for your subject is a part of grabbing your students' attention, it's certainly not the only thing. Students will not respond positively to your teaching just because *you* like the subject that you are teaching. Students often have a fence that they put up if they feel that they are working for the benefit of others. So, the trick is to figure out a way to either make whatever it is that you are trying to teach fun, or figure out a way for the students to take ownership of what you are teaching.

When you are asking a question, don't just call on those with their hands up. Mix it up by calling on those with their hands down. Give them time to give a response, if not the correct answer. Perhaps give them a hint. If they give a response, figure out a way to connect the response with the actual correct answer. Keep your body language positive and encourage the student. The next time, he will feel less threatened to respond and will know that he has something to contribute to the class. If only the same students are allowed to participate, why wouldn't the others feel apathetic toward the class?

Be sure to give any student you've called upon the time to respond with an answer. Most teachers give students less than two seconds before they give the answer themselves, or pass the question along to another student. (Time yourself once!) Don't disengage the synapse in a student's brain before it has a chance to take place.

The moment a student you did not call on interrupts with an answer, stop the class and explain that when an answer is blurted out of turn, everyone in the class will lose the opportunity to know the correct answer and have it stick in their brains. Students dig the explanation of the synapse "thing" that goes on in the brain, and they will better understand why they should refrain from interrupting. This is a very positive way to manage your classroom and build student ownership, while all along snuffing out student apathy.

He who wishes to secure the good of others has already secured his own.

—Confucius

Teaching is an ego-less profession. One where your main goal is to not only pass on all of your knowledge to your students, but also to see that your students take that knowledge to the next level to become even more successful than you.

This same comfort level we teachers have with student success must also extend to the success of our fellow educators. Often, when a teacher has a great idea, a sure fire way to teach students effectively, he is reluctant to share this idea with other teachers in case they use this idea to become more successful. *Wow!* What is our mission as a teacher—to bask in isolated satisfaction, or to build a better world by educating the next generation of citizens? This may include giving out all of your ideas, methods, lessons, handouts, etc. to fellow teachers...and that's okay.

Familiarity breeds contempt.

—Proverb

It's okay to be friendly with your students, but never familiar. We are there for our students to be their teacher, counselor, advisor, etc., not to be their friend. How can you discipline a friend? Friends do not give homework or deny privileges. Friends are people students complain to about their teachers! Friends do not give rules, and students know that teachers without rules are teachers who do not care. Students like the idea of the teacher being in charge of the class, on a level above them. This division must be clear, and once it is, students will be in an environment where they can learn.

Students will try several different angles to approach you and dig into business that is not yours to share. A simple, "That is a question you should not ask a teacher," or "The answer to that is something I'm not able to share with you or any student," will draw a line that students will quickly learn they are not to cross in the future. Accordingly, it's up to you as the teacher to not get into the students' business, which is not yours as well. It's friendly to ask if the student had a good weekend, but too familiar to ask if they went to the dance and who they took.

Drawing the line between friendliness and familiarity is sometimes more difficult for teachers who have more contact with the students, such as a coach or music teacher. But no matter who you are and no matter what you do, "familiarity breeds contempt." This is especially true with a person who is in charge of others. If you want to be able to stay in charge, contempt is the one thing that will cause you to lose this position. Remember, you are professional because *you* are, not because your students are.

The trouble with most of us is that we would rather be ruined by praise than saved by criticism.

—N. V. Peale

It's very common to sugar coat a problem a student is having because we can empathize with him or her. Although empathy is a great attribute to have, is your handling of this situation benefiting the student in the long run? Be up-front with your students when teaching and guiding them, but never be nasty or discourteous.

It's a process

An out-of-control day can happen to even veteran teachers on any day of any year of their teaching careers if their classroom management skills do not stay sharp. Effective classroom management is an ongoing process. Times change, students change and ideas change. Educational philosophy changes. Even the physical environment of the classroom changes; consider the impact of computers and other technologies.

2 Developing the Complete Child

It seems that every time a problem is addressed in education, it always requires millions of dollars to fix. But the very best things in life—including building moral character in our students—cost very little or even nothing at all. As music educators, we are in a unique position to keep vigil over the actions of our students and guide them down the right path in life.

The way to behave in society isn't a concept that magically enters a person's mind and body. It requires experience, conversing with others and allowing for mistakes. Unfortunately, the very social interaction that teaches these principles is on the decline. Only a short time ago, the neighborhood kids would have to meet in the street to play a game of kickball or kick-the-can. Today, kids have access to the entire universe from their own rooms. They can converse with people all over the world without ever having any meaningful social interaction with them.

This is where we come in. At its core, choral singing is a study of interactions: student-to-teacher interaction, student-to-student interaction and chorus-to-audience interaction. Since our chorus class is designed around social interaction, what better venue and outlet to begin teaching character than our classroom?

You learn more from your losses than you do from your wins.

—Vince Lombardi

Which do you remember more: the answers you got right on an important test, or those you didn't? Do you ever misspell a word that you once misspelled, to your embarrassment? By making mistakes a part of your class, the students will become more actively engaged and the thought process will thrive.

The same is true for mistakes students may make on a larger scale throughout their school career and throughout life's journey. Even though the student's mistake may be bigger, and the consequence more punitive, it's still an event where learning can take place; hopefully enough learning to prevent a terrible mistake. School is a safe, controlled environment that prepares our students for the "real world." If they make a big mistake in school and pay the price, the hope is that they won't make the same mistake, much less a bigger one, in the future, when their actions will have much harsher consequences.

Taking care of our own problems

When our students get in trouble or disobey one of the rules, it's tempting to call their parents or send them to the office to take care of the problem. But, when you send the problem to a third party, misinformation can cause the problem to become even worse. With the exception of major violations (which will be address in Chapter 3), you may want to take care of the problem yourself, especially if you have a good rapport with the students.

You can gain your students' respect by showing that you are strong enough to deal with situations without passing them on to other people. But most importantly, you are teaching your students to be responsible for their behavior by demonstrating your own responsibility in a difficult situation. When it's time for your students to take on responsibility for their behavior, they will respect you and listen to you more if they saw your excellent example first.

Don't make a mountain out of a molehill

Work to solve the problem at hand instead of manufacturing a bigger problem. Not only does this preserve your valuable time and effort, it shows your students that you are a rational person and wish to focus on the task at hand instead of making it bigger than it is. Just as you wouldn't put a Band-Aid® on a broken arm, you stand a better chance of solving a problem or task if you address the actual problem. On the other hand, if there is a cut and it can be fixed with only a Band-Aid®, then do it! However, if the student breaks a bone, get a doctor to set it in a cast! If it's necessary, don't hesitate to get professional assistance immediately.

Our character is what we do when we think no one is looking.

—H. Jackson Brown, Jr.

Even better still, if you can prevent students from getting a cut or breaking their bones in the first place by convincing them of how to keep their skin and bones healthy, then do it! Any teacher can lay down a punishment when a student breaks a rule. However, it takes quite a teacher to help a student develop his own character so that he feels no need to break the rules.

The more uncivilized the man, the surer he is that he knows what is right and what is wrong.

—Mencken

Early on, most of us have an innate sense of right and wrong. As we get older, that sense can be corrupted or strengthened. As your students' teacher, you have a great power to make a change in so many of their lives, and guiding your students to be honest is one of the greatest things you can do for them!

Every child hopes that their teachers will eventually run out of advice.

—Anon.

Most of the time, children and adolescents do not show outward expression when you are speaking to them. However, do not fool yourself...they can hear everything you are saying! So any time you say anything to anyone (of any age) think before you speak, because everything you say has a major impact on those who are listening. They may remember something you said for a very, very long time. Wouldn't it be wonderful if what you said had a positive impact on that person forever? You have that opportunity each and every time you deal with your students.

The kindness planned for tomorrow doesn't count today.

—Anon.

When you take the time to call home or write a letter about something a child did *well* in your class, it has a stronger, more binding impact than calling or writing about something mischievous a child did. When you write a short note or letter to your students, they will often save it for a long time and refer to it later. You may have been the only teacher who ever took the time to do this, and the impact will be tremendous!

Even if you simply leave a message, it has a positive effect on the students and their parents and will better open the communication with both parties as you work to guide the student. Do it immediately!

Some students will do anything for a good grade, except work for it.

—Anon.

Students in school learn very fast that it's easier to cheat to get their assignments or homework completed. Students also learn very quickly that there may be no possible way that they could get caught by a teacher if they cheat on their work or even a test, so they just simply cheat. Cheating makes perfect sense for a student who is not going to get caught, so what is the problem?

Students need to hear from someone who they look up to that there *is* a problem; that it's wrong to cheat. They need to be told that not getting caught doesn't make cheating okay. Mostly, they need to be instilled with the fact that they are only cheating themselves. Sure, they have probably heard this time after time, but each time they hear it, the students will think at least twice about cheating.

Have you ever been playing a game, whether it's dodgeball, kickball, or even a board game, where someone always has to cheat? Do you remember how frustrating it is—the cheater acting like a baby and spoiling the game for everyone? Can you imagine how boring a baseball game would be if one team was allowed three outs and the other four? What kind of game would that be? We all understand that in any game, all things being equal, someone has to win and someone has to lose. Yet even when we lose, it's comforting to know that everything was fair and square.

The same thing is true when you are doing your homework or taking a test. If you know that you worked hard and took the time to complete an assignment, or studied your guts out to prepare for a test, you are usually satisfied with the score, even if you would rather it be higher. And if you are dissatisfied, you usually are better prepared next time because you learned from your failure. However, if you cheat, you don't get a feeling of satisfaction, and you certainly don't learn anything except that you got away with cheating, which deep down, makes anyone feel sick to their stomach.

A juvenile delinquent gives up stealing bases when he starts stealing cars.

—Anon.

Early on, children learn that they shouldn't take something that doesn't belong to them. In middle school, teachers must work with students to expand the definition of "what doesn't belong to them." Many students in middle school work in the lunchroom or student store, collect money for charities, etc. They should learn that it's just as much stealing when they give extra food to their friends in the lunch line. They should learn that it's just as much stealing when they give a donut to a friend or spend money collected for a charity on a vending machine.

Not taking what doesn't belong to you also includes debunking the "finder's keepers, loser's weepers" rhyme. Share with your students how good it feels to give an item back to someone who dropped it. Encourage your students to help a fellow student retrieve something he or she dropped or lost; the response you receive for this kindness will make one feel good. This may seem corny, but it's definitely part of guiding your students along the right track. Honesty is contagious!

No one has a good enough memory to make a successful liar.

—Abraham Lincoln

Children can learn very quickly that it's easy to tell a lie in order to get out of a situation, or to make their life seem easier for the time being, and they may not even get caught. But as with stealing, getting away with it doesn't make it the right thing to do.

You can teach your students that if they tell even one lie, they must remember that lie over and over with so many different people that eventually they are going to get caught, and that is a sick feeling! It only takes one lie before a person is branded as a liar. Students need to be told that although telling the truth may initially get you in trouble with a friend or turn people against you, the truth will impart you with a sense of freedom and others will respect your honesty in the long run. Students, indeed people in general, tend to think in the short term. We should guide our students that there are long-term consequences to lying, and they do not want that on their conscience. Simply tell the truth, and everything eventually will fall into place.

Now what about telling a white lie? Students need to know the difference between lying to deceive and making a statement that you don't necessarily agree with in order to make someone feel better. Think back to a school project that took you weeks to complete; a school project that in hindsight may have fallen a little short on idea and implementation. When asked how they liked it, your parents inevitably replied, "That's the coolest thing on the planet!" Were they lying when they said that? Your parents appreciated the fact that you spent a long time on something, which is what mattered most to them, so they told you that the project was wonderful. It really doesn't take a rocket scientist to discern between making a statement to deceive and making a statement to uplift another.

The opportunity to sing in a beautifully sounding choir is the result of consistent dedication, commitment and love for the music, as well as positive interaction between each chorus member. There is no way to steal to learn how to read music, there is no way to cheat to learn how to sing beautifully, and there is no way to lie to bring it all together. Choral students learn that it's not necessary to cheat, steal or lie to get a major feeling of accomplishment. Hopefully, with your guidance, they can transfer this to other areas in their lives.

Few things can help an individual more than to place responsibility on him, and to let him know that you trust him.

—Booker T. Washington

Singing in a chorus is work unto itself, but what else can we do to instill a work ethic in our students? One way is simply placing meaningful responsibility on your students and trusting them. You may find that the student who you thought would be least likely to accept and follow-through on a responsibility may be the very student who comes through the most. Further, you may be the only teacher who offers this particular student any responsibility, and she may be eager to prove herself up to the challenge.

A true leader always has a burning desire to give back to the community.

—Anon.

Another way we can help our students become productive citizens is to create opportunities for them to be involved in their community. Students can file papers, enter data on the computer or catalog choral music. They also love to wash windows, empty the garbage or recycle bin, vacuum or mop the floor, dust, and straighten the room. Not only does it give them a sense of responsibility and ownership, it will encourage the students to police themselves. They will work to see that the room stays clean and snuff out problems before they begin, such as students disposing of their gum on the floor rather than in its proper place. When students have an input on the physical grounds of the school, they will certainly take better care of the facility.

If we are able to get students involved in community service with the use of their choral singing, great! If the students get the sense that they can make the world a better place through the use of their talents, they will surely do just that! Students can also build their character by singing at a nursing home or other charitable community events, going to your feeder elementary schools to sing or help with school activities, or organizing a community cleanup. Any way you can get involved with your students to help them be an important part of the community not only develops their character but also helps build camaraderie between the members of the chorus.

We don't stop playing because we grow old, we grow old because we stop playing.

—Herbert Spencer

Playing games also builds a camaraderie and you can have the students experience many of the very things you are trying to teach while they are playing, including learning right from wrong, following rules, instilling a work habit, and, especially, developing social interaction and building people skills. You can play a game of kickball with your class—the sopranos and basses against the altos and tenors, for example. You can play board games as well, which have the same effect as more physical games. You can utilize games in your classroom to help aide what you are teaching, whether you make up new games or incorporate games the students already know, such as music baseball. (The students are divided into teams and each question is worth a base. Get students involved keeping score, etc.) There are many resources for musical games you can play with your classes, so the sky is the limit!

There are no uninteresting things; there are only uninterested people.

—Chesterton

When you take an interest in your students' other academic studies and school work, it shows that you care about them as students first, and that you do not think that your class is the end-all of the world.

Strike while the iron is hot.

—Proverb

Every year, there seems to be at least one student who is a thorn in your side. It seems that no matter what you do, it has no effect on the student. Usually the case comes down to the student seeking attention from anyone, anywhere, at any cost. This is where the teacher needs to be on top of the situation, always one step ahead of the student.

Working with a student like this is similar to a blacksmith working with iron. If the iron is cool, you can pound it and pound it, but it will neither form nor bend, only break. Only when the iron is hot enough can it be formed. Indeed, the timing has to be just right, and you have to be very careful when you are working with hot iron.

As a teacher working with a difficult student, you must find the best time to pound your help into the student—but only when they are ready to hear it. As hard as it is at times, try to avoid pounding and pounding when nothing is going to form or bend anyway. When the difficult student is doing something well, a teacher may have a tendency to think that the student is too cool or doesn't want positive attention. This is not true! The difficult student is testing to see if you are aware enough to see that he is doing something constructive. It is up to you to acknowledge any good coming from the student. If appropriate, write a little note to the student explaining what a great job he did so that he has something to physically latch onto when he did something well.

And just as the blacksmith has to pound, bend and shape over and over while the iron is hot, the teacher must do the same. The iron is not going to form with one pound, and the difficult student is not going to change overnight. It will take a patient and consistent effort on the teacher's part.

Advise your student's career appropriately

There will come a time when the development of a student in your class will be better served by a different class. Always be attune to what is in the best interest of each student and give her the latitude to move to a different class if that is what's required. Even though choral directors may think the world revolves around music, this student's world may not. She may come back to you later and thank you for caring more about her as a person and advising her in such an unselfish way.

On the other hand, there may be a time when it's best for a student to be in your class, even though you may not want her there because her presence makes things more difficult. If this is the case, keep her and work with her. Both the teacher and the student will benefit in the long run.

Develop a variety of non-musical skills with your students

Music requires many skills which the students need to develop to become a better person and successful in today's society. Although you are a teacher of music, you are in a unique position to help the students to develop non-music skills such as leadership roles, citizenship, working with each other, etc. Take this honor seriously and treat it with the respect it deserves!

At school, we first learn to read, and then we read to learn.

—Anon.

You can read stories or poetry with your students that pertain to building character to get them thinking about what is the right thing to do. Design a lesson around the story—don't just read the stories and leave it at that. Discuss what the stories mean and what the point is. It's sometimes miraculous how much insight the students have, and how much they can add to your class to help their fellow students become better people. Some excellent examples include:

- "Mr. Vinegar seeks His Fortune," retold by James Baldwin
- "Good and Bad Children," by Robert Louis Stevenson
- "If," by Rudyard Kipling
- "The King and His Hawk," retold by James Baldwin
- "The Little Red Hen," retold by Penrhyn W. Coussens
- "The Tortise and the Hare," by Aesop
- "The Hero of Indian Cliff," adapted by C. H. Claudy
- "Mother Theresa," retold by William J. Bennett
- "The Boy Who Cried 'Wolf,'" by Aesop
- "The Honest Woodman," adapted from Emilie Poulsson[1]

---

[1] The first three stories can be found in *The Book of Virtues*, edited by William J. Bennett and published by Simon & Schuster. All other stories can be found in Mr. Bennett's *The Children's Treasury of Virtues*, also published by Simon & Schuster.

Do the Right Thing: Responses to Major Problems

3

What happens when there is "Trouble in Paradise," "Trouble in River City," or just plain-old trouble with your choral program or students? Everyone has a bad day here and there, but sometimes, trouble goes beyond that, leaving you to deal with and respond to a major problem. On top of the problem itself, how you respond to the problem will set a precedent for future students and can ward off the same problem or other potential problems in the future.

The problem is not that there are problems. The problem is expecting otherwise and thinking that having a problem is a problem.

—Theodore Rubin

Many times, major problems happen at the worst possible time, and what seems like an isolated incident can have ramifications on the entire class. This is especially true for a chorus teacher or coach if your "star singer" or "star player" is the one in trouble. Although dealing with the infraction may be a cut-and-dry case, dealing with major problems can take its emotional toll. You have to deal with the impact of this student's presence, or lack thereof, on the group as a whole. You also have to deal with any emotional connection you may have with this student, and the feeling that you had a hand in removing the student from the only environment that may be able to guide him or her toward a better life—your classroom. It is, however, essential that you put emotions to the side, and use your best judgment and seek higher advice to help guide your decision.

There are many ways to react to major infractions:

- Let the problem slide and hope it will go away
- Give the student a "pass" because this was the first major infraction
- Punish but not remove the student because this is the only environment you feel can help him
- Punish but not remove the student because "the team will suffer"
- Punish the student by having him sit out a game or concert
- Punish the student by taking away a major privilege (i.e. travel)
- Punish and remove the student from the team for his own good
- Punish and remove the student from the team to set an example

This list may be the tip of the iceberg of your options, especially if the school administration, or even the police department, is involved. To further muddy the situation, teachers who have a rapport or (previous) mutual respect with the student who broke a major rule can sometimes be emotionally attached and worry about making the correct decision when dealing with the student.

Planes, trains and automobiles

When dealing with a major problem, consider the philosophical differences between a Japanese car assembly plant and an American car assembly plant. When there is a problem on a Japanese assembly line, it goes into shut-down mode and all of the experts on hand are called to the problem until it's solved. When, and only when, a solution to the problem is found and implemented by the experts is work resumed. The production shut down may last for quite a while and the production of cars will be lower for the day, but the problem will be solved and the plant will be ready to go. When there is a problem on an American assembly line, it keeps going, ensuring that they can keep "pumping out" cars to the dealers. After weeks, months, or even years, the problem comes to the attention of enough people that a recall is ordered. This requires all car owners to take their cars to their respective dealers in order for the problem to be fixed, at a greater cost to the manufacturer over the long run.

A similar decision is yours to make if you get a flat tire while you are driving. You can stop the car, put on a spare and proceed, or you can continue driving on the flat until you reach your destination or a service station. By putting on the spare, you invested some time, but you've fixed the problem and may move on. (Of course, you eventually have to fix the original tire, but you get the gist.) If you continue driving, you may discover that you did more damage to the car, which isn't made to be driven on a flat tire, and now must spend even more time and money to get the car back to normal.

Whenever there is a small problem in the classroom, i.e. excessive talking or a scuffle, that you haven't been able to solve with non-verbal behaviors, it's best to stop the class—no matter what you are doing—and deal with the problem. Once the problem is solved, the class can go on. If, instead, you ignore the problem, the student who broke the rule will get the sense that it was perfectly fine to do so because it wasn't addressed immediately. Others in the class will, by extension, see that it's okay to break the rules because nothing will come of it. In this scenario, as your class gets away from you so too does your respect and credibility. The same logic follows for addressing major problems. (There are times when a teacher may decide that the best thing to do is keep the class moving and deal with the problem later. If this is the case, and you truly feel that this is best for all involved, do it.)

Examples of infractions

Major problems generally fall into one of three categories:

1. Infractions which can stop the flow of the class

2. Infractions which can harm the student or school property

3. Infractions which can harm others' safety

Examples of each and suggestions for dealing with the problem behaviors follow.

1. Infractions which can stop the flow of the class

Fighting—Two students are scuffling in your class, but both stop soon after they are told to by the teacher. Being cautious of your physical safety, you should do your best to separate the students or hold one them back. Another student may try to hold back the other student.

Profanity—A student swears in your class while you are teaching. Answer the profanity with, "It's none of my business if you use that kind of language on your own time, but it's not to be used on our time."

2. Infractions which can harm a student or school property

Vandalism—A student is caught vandalizing school property (i.e. a computer, pictures on the wall, a musical instrument, etc.). Vandalism is usually covered by the school rules and is therefore dealt with by the school administration, who may chose to file a police report. Regardless of the past contributions of this student, the act of destroying property shows that either the student doesn't care about or respect his surroundings, or he feels that he is immune from any punishment. Either way, for the student's benefit, he must be referred to the administration, and you should excuse him from your team or program.

Possession of Alcohol/Drugs—You catch a group of students drinking while out of town on tour. Drinking is against the law for a minor and should be dealt with as such. Involvement of the student's parents and the school administration is a necessity, both to set the proper example for your program and to ensure that the student receives treatment.

3. Infractions which can harm others' safety

This category includes serious offenses like arson, assault and possession of a firearm or other weapon. In addition to creating situations that endanger the lives of those around them, each of these is a criminal act. The crime must be reported to the police and the student must face the consequences of these potentially deadly behaviors. It's difficult for any teacher to see his or her student facing such dire consequences but you must put your responsibility for the safety of all your students first.

4 Yin and Yang in the Choral Classroom

One of the great symbols is the yin and yang. According to Chinese theory, it symbolizes two forces in the universe. The yin is the passive, negative force, and the yang is the active, positive force. The Chinese believe that wise people will detect these forces in the seasons, in their food, and so on, and will regulate their lives accordingly. Expanding on this theory of opposites, we notice that for fire there is water, for sky there is earth, for dark there is light, for up there is down.

If teachers take this theory of opposites and put it to use in their classrooms, they will regulate their teaching accordingly and find a balance previously thought impossible when dealing with the varied personalities they teach throughout a lifetime. If choral directors take this theory into their conducting, they will experience unprecedented musical success. If vocal instructors apply this theory, their singers will open new paths to technical and musical success.

I do not know the key to success, but the key to failure is trying to please everybody.

—Bill Cosby

Trying to please everyone becomes even harder when "everyone" includes 300+ choral students, their parents, the administration, fellow teachers, the community, and even yourself. The law of averages, not to mention experience, say that no matter how hard you try you will *not* be able to please everybody. Spending your time and energy to do so is most certainly a waste of everyone's time, especially yours! Instead, put the yin and yang theory into practice.

Leaders are in their positions because somebody put them there. Leaders lead people who, for the most part, have a desire to be led. The vast majority of people being led want to be dealt with fairly but understand that they are not going to get their way all of the time. If you are making a decision based on the well being of the entire class, make it. That is your leadership role as the teacher. If you are making a decision based on your leadership skills as a chorus director, make it. That is your role as a chorus director. If the buck stops with you as the leader on a school committee, make it, because that is your role.

As long as you honestly took many factors into consideration with your students, your choral program or your committee, people understand that the person in the leadership role has to make the final decision. There will be a few people who express their dissatisfaction. However, deep down, if they know you are fair and have conviction in your decision, they will respect you as well as your decision. If you've made a decision you feel is totally fair, honest, and for the benefit of the people you are leading, stick with it! Avoid caving to the initial protests and think of the big picture. Know that with any tough decision often comes criticism, but that mustn't stop you from making a decision. Consider this baseball analogy:

> You are watching a baseball game and in the bottom of the third inning, a runner is stealing second. The catcher throws, and bang, the umpire has to make a call, fast. In that split second, the umpire very quickly comes to the decision that the runner has been tagged out. The umpire doesn't necessarily have to make the correct call (although replays show that the umpire is correct over 98% of the time) but he has to be *sure* of his call. Here's why: First, the runner throws up his arms in disgust because he thought for sure that he was safe. While he is pleading his case, the manager comes running toward second base arguing his case in a most animated way. Then, the 50,000 people in the stands loudly and rudely voice their opinions.

Perhaps the umpire is thinking deep down inside that the runner could have been safe, but this is not to be displayed in any way, shape, or form to the players, coaches, and fans. Either the runner is out or he is safe. He was called out, and that is that. After the protesting, arguing and body gestures, the game goes on. Everyone on the team and in the stadium knows that it's the umpire's job to make the calls as accurately and fairly as he is capable of doing. Everyone (even the umpire himself) understands that there are going to be a few missed calls every now and then. But nobody wants to see the umpire scratch his head and adopt a look of complete indecision while the players, coaches and fans are protesting. If the umpire changed his mind and announced that the runner was indeed safe, short-term happiness would erupt. However, all respect for the umpire would be lost for the rest of his career because of his indecisiveness. And that includes the respect of those who benefited from the reversed call. If this happened all of the time, the game of baseball would be in a shambles and would ultimately cease to function.

When your students are agitated, be calm and still

An out-of-control class or student is a lot like fire. Although there are times when you have to fight fire with fire, it's best to try to douse fire with water first. Your calm, still demeanor will wash over the class, quieting their behavior and opening a channel for more effective communication; communication which was, after all, the ultimate purpose of their out-of-control behavior.

Amigo, compadre, good buddy, old pal

One of the first mistakes that all teachers make is thinking that if they put themselves on the level of the students, reason with them and act "buddy-buddy," the students will respond to their teaching. Nothing is further from the truth. Students know when a teacher is trying too hard to be their buddy. They also know that this is not an effective way for them to learn. The old adage "the stricter you are, the better your students," still has its place in today's classroom.

We assume that being successful creates fun, but that is backwards. By having fun, we free up our best resources. So the truth is, it's fun that creates success.

—Clifford C. Kuhn

Sometimes we take our lives so seriously that we forget to have fun with what we are doing. When we are having fun at what we do, we usually succeed because there is no burden in what we are doing. Having fun also brings out the best in people. If you are struggling in everything that you do, it's not fun, even when you get things accomplished. So lighten up at times and have fun with your students while you are learning!

Ask singers to sing, and you can't get them to start; don't ask them to sing, and you can't get them to stop.

—Horace

If you tell your students to "lift their soft palate," you will be left with 50 or 100 or even 300 interpretations of "lift." If, instead, you simply *demonstrate* how to take in a breath which causes the soft palate to lift, the choral students will universally understand what to do and you will have 50 or 100 or even 300 people doing the same thing at the same time. Say less, do more. It's a more exciting—and more effective—way to learn.

The absence of a disciplinarian will help to guide self-discipline

There are times when it's appropriate for the teacher to step back and allow the students to self-govern their problems. You may be there to guide them, but when the students come up with their own solutions to their own problems the lessons will be more effective and the benefits longer-lasting.

The slower you go, the faster you learn

This is especially true when explaining a difficult task or working on difficult passages in the music. If you just "plow through" something, most people will get a feeling of success, even though no real learning is taking place. Don't make this mistake. Take the time it takes to learn something thoroughly.

Part Two

Teaching Music—The Unique Challenges

5 Managing Your Rehearsal for Sanity...and Success!

The classroom management tools presented in Chapter 1 are effective whether you are teaching biology, choir or shop, but for each different classroom environment, there are unique classroom management challenges. The same goes for the choral rehearsal.

The first person gets the oyster, the second person gets the shell.

—Andrew Carnegie

Begin your rehearsal on time! No matter the consequences of their punctuality, or lack thereof, your students will be a reflection of your example. How many times do you show up for a meeting or a rehearsal and the person in charge doesn't begin on time? It gives you the signal that either the person in charge is not organized or the meeting is not really important. The same is true for your rehearsal.

Make it a habit to begin the class with singing. You may want to even begin your warm-up exercises as the students walk in and before the bell rings. It shows that singing is the most important event in the chorus room! Also, if there are times when the class is getting out of control and the students will not stop talking, get them up and singing, even if it's a time when you wanted to be explaining something. They will then be singing instead of talking. Also, it will save you from giving the "get quiet" lecture. Save any announcements until an appropriate time during the middle of the rehearsal or at the end of the rehearsal. The class will listen to them better and you will lose less momentum than if you give your announcements at the beginning of the period.

The trouble with most people is that they listen with their mouths.

—Proverb

An easy, non-threatening way to get the class to stop their activities and focus on you is to say any of the following:

1. Clap once if you can hear me.
2. Clap two times if you can hear me.
3. Clap three times and keep your eyes on me.
4. Touch your elbows.
5. Whisper, "I'm listening."

The *Addams Family* is another fun, non-verbal way to get the attention of the class, or even an entire auditorium.

1. Play the first four notes of the *Addams Family* theme (sol, la, ti, do) on the piano (two hands, two octaves apart)
2. Guide the students to clap or snap twice
3. Play the next phrase—sol, la, ti, do—starting a whole step higher
4. Guide the students to clap or snap twice
5. Repeat the phrase from Step 3 twice, followed by the original four notes
6. Guide the class to clap or snap twice and every eye will be on you!

When utilizing any of these non-verbal attention getters, be sure to move to your lesson immediately after getting the group's attention. Launching into a lecture about their behavior only diminishes the effectiveness of this exercise.

Failure is only the opportunity to begin again more intelligently.

—Henry Ford

When the class enters in a disorderly fashion, direct them to leave the room. (It's best if you have a plan for where the students should line up—in a straight line, a square, separate lines, etc.) Once the students are "at attention," explain that you were not satisfied with the way they entered the room and you expect them to enter in the proper manner. After this short but firm speech, command: "I will give you another chance. Please enter the room quickly and quietly, without talking."

Raise your hand when asking a question

When you are asking a question that is open to anyone in the class, raise *your* hand (almost like taking an oath) and scan the room before you call on a student. When you are calling on a student, firmly point to the student as you call her name.

The quality of an individual is reflected in the standards they set for themselves.

—Ray Kroc

The best way to manage a choral rehearsal is to direct the choir as a single entity, rather than trying to direct each and every student. Seventy against one are tough odds to overcome, but one against (or with!) one is manageable for anyone. It's very common to interpret the behavior of individual students as the behavior of the choir as a whole. In other words, if one student is talking, we tend to interpret this as the whole choir talking. If one student is not standing up tall, we focus on that one student and interpret it as the whole choir slouching. Do not make this mistake! Just take care of the individual problem and move on.

If you have a cut on your arm that is painful, it's hard to think of anything else. Thankfully, our entire body doesn't focus its energy on that one cut, for it has other, more important activities to do, like keeping our heart beating and lungs breathing to supply blood and oxygen for the rest of the body. The same is true for the chorus. If there are one or two individuals causing a problem, don't take it out on the whole choir. Do not even acknowledge it to the whole choir. Just as your body takes care of the cut on your arm as quickly and painlessly as it is able, find ways to take care of the small problem in the choir as quickly and painlessly as you are able.

Stop the music!

If you're playing the piano during the rehearsal and see one or two students off task, simply stare directly at the students and stop what you are doing. The abrupt stop of the flow of the music will grab everyone's attention, especially those not on task. *Do not say anything!* The students who are the most off task will shape up the most, and everyone else will give themselves a quick gut-check. Everyone will look directly at you and those who were daydreaming instead of singing attentively will get back on task.

This very simple tool does so many things in such a short period of time:

1. Non-verbal cues show both parties that you are in control and you are respectful. Students have no respect for a teacher who seems oblivious to the problems going on in the classroom.

2. It shows that you are able to isolate and take care of the problem without penalizing other students.

3. It shows that you care about the students in a way that you don't have to shout or humiliate a student for talking in the class. They will respect you more because you took care of the problem in a non-threatening way.

4. It gives each student the feeling that they had better think twice before they get off task because the teacher will immediately spot the problem.

5. It actually lightens the class even though the students become more on task. And students singing in a chorus must have an internal sense of freedom to perform at their maximum level.

It's not the load that breaks you down, it's the way you carry it.

—Lena Horne

Sometimes an event may have taken place in school the previous hour and the students want to talk about it. Perhaps the students want to catch up with their friends after the weekend. There may be a time when it's best to let the students have time to talk, but this shouldn't last more than a minute or two. You may want to move to the side of the class (instead of in front of) as if to show that you are still there, aware of the talking going on, and giving your approval (provided you have decided that the talking is necessary for the students to have closure of a previous event).

If it's a case of students simply talking out of control or when it's time for the class to begin, stand statue-like in front of the class until the students stop talking. You will be extremely surprised how quickly this will happen. Often teachers allow less than ten seconds to elapse before they start yelling for their students to be quiet. If you give the students a few seconds (up to 30-45), they will eventually get quiet on their own. This is much better because they got quiet and on task on their terms and will cooperate more during the rehearsal. Do not reinforce or give verbal attention to negative behavior, which includes the class talking beyond their boundary.

If the entire class seems to be off task, talking, or moving all over the place (which is a frequent happening in the middle school classroom), command the class to "Freeze!" For one reason or another, the students stop moving and (as a bonus) stop talking! While they are "frozen," ask the students to take their places (in their seats or on the risers) quietly without talking. It's magical! You took care of the problem without blowing your top and without threatening any student or the class as a whole. Further, it shows that *you* are ultimately in control of the class and the students will respond to you better while you are teaching.

You can tell whether a man is clever by his answers. You can tell whether a man is wise by his questions.

—Mahfouz Naguib

Students are generally conditioned to respond to direction with various delay tactics. From asking you to repeat the question or instruction to throwing out "Start at measure 17?" or "Where are we again?", the class must be broken of this habit.

Often the teacher will let the student off the hook by allowing a student who knows the answer to give a response and bail out the other student. This is a sure way to reward the students who don't pay attention, and cause you to lose the respect of those who do.

The first time a delay tactic is used, explain to the class that such delay tactics lead to making excuses in everyday life and ultimately accomplishing nothing, and are not acceptable in your class. If, after this explanation, a student asks you to repeat the question, guide the *student* to repeat the question, because chances are she heard something. This shows that it was the question that was important, and your nurturing guidance helps spare the student any humiliation. Perhaps it may be necessary to ask another student if he can help his friend recall the question (not the answer). Once the question has been established, the chosen student must be directly responsible for answering it herself. Again, the best teacher will guide the student while she is answering the question. Remember, the goal isn't to pull a "gotcha!" on the student. This approach will definitely take longer the first few times a delay tactic is used, but remember that you are ultimately investing in the future, avoiding delays and saving time in the long run.

If a student says, "Start at measure 17?," he may be expecting a few minutes respite from singing as you rattle off the "why it's important for you to pay attention" lecture that so many teachers use. Instead of wasting your valuable rehearsal time, you can best handle this by saying, "That's exactly right, now go!" It will actually encourage the student and help him sing, play or answer any question better. If a student says, "I don't know where we are," it may be a good time to use humor. Consider saying, "Neither do I, can you help me?" Or, if it's a time to be firmer, you may say, "The same place we've been the last three times." This is a less threatening, yet compelling way to tell the student to pay attention. Once again, take the time to explain to the students to get out of the habit of delaying, which leads to making excuses. They will work harder and become better equipped for life.

The mediocre teacher tells. The good teacher explains. The superior teacher demonstrates. The great teacher inspires.

—William Arthur Ward

If you inspire your students, they will motivate themselves, allowing great lifelong learning to happen. Even greater achievements and accomplishments will take place, as your students will become self-learners who are turned on to learning. Once this happens, the world is at their doorstep, and in the end, the world will be better because of your inspiration! Oftentimes, teachers feel that motivation is the key to learning. It definitely is! However, many teachers and coaches spend a great deal of their energy motivating a student, class or team. As hard as you try, you are not actually motivating anyone because motivation comes from within. You can set the stage for motivating, you can help students or classes to motivate themselves, but in the end, motivation has to come from within each individual.

Think of motivation as hunger and think of learning as eating. You cannot make a person hungry because hunger comes from within. Further, you cannot make a person eat because the person has to physically chew and swallow. You can yell and scream all you want to try to make a person hungry, but it will be to no avail. You can, however, set the stage for a person to become hungry. There is a great chance that if you display the most delicious food available in the most beautiful setting available, a person will suddenly become hungry. Now that he is hungry, it's now up to *him* to eat. You can offer the plate, the utensils, and even show him how to eat, but *he* is ultimately in charge of eating now that he's hungry. The exact same thing is true for motivation and learning.

Since success can breed motivation, create a motivational growth pattern by letting your students experience success. Always try to capitalize on any accomplishments! Every time you do this, the students will feel more upright and will motivate themselves. This will, in turn, lead to more success which will, of course, motivate the students even more. It's a growth pattern similar to building a skyscraper. You begin with a firm foundation and keep building up and up from there. Just as building projects run into snags, your progress will run into snags. However, don't let anger or frustration get in the way of progress. Or if you feel frustrated, at least keep it from showing to the students. Deal with it on your own, but don't let the students become a part of the problem. Help them be part of the solution.

Be a choral director, not a choral corrector.

—Rodney Eichenberger

The moment something doesn't go as you planned in your rehearsal is most likely the moment when you'll want to fix the problem. What is the first thing most of us say to fix the problem? We verbalize it, making everyone aware of the problem and ensuring that they're thinking about it. Now, when you ask the choir to go back, the problem may have gotten even worse. Why? Because you called attention to the problem not the solution. Instead of verbalizing the problem, always allow the choral students to fix the problem by solving it themselves. First, it will give them ownership of the chorus, and second, identifying and solving their own problems will create a motivational growth pattern. In turn, this will train the choral student to develop good listening skills and help elevate their musicianship to a higher level.

Let's say you went back and gave the choral students the latitude to identify and correct the musical problem and they didn't fix it the first time around. Don't say anything. Give the body language or the correct choral gesture and direction to enable the students to solve the problem. Do *not* tell them where to begin...they will know. And if they don't know the first couple of times you use this technique, they will catch on very, very quickly the next time! This saves a great deal of time down the road and it helps you keep the students on task more often.

Listen to yourself each time you run a rehearsal. You will be surprised at how much wasted mumble-jumble verbiage comes from your mouth! How would *you* respond during a choral rehearsal if you were the singer and a director verbalized each and every mistake you made? Would you be able to solve the problem without the director verbalizing the problem? Probably so. So why shouldn't your students be offered the chance to do the same? The less you say, the more the choral students will take ownership of the music and their responsibility to learn.

Focus with fun

A rhythmic fugue game like the one that follows is an enthusiastic way to get a class focused and get the students physically involved and mentally alert. The leader (usually the teacher until the students quickly catch on) claps a four-beat pattern, such as clapping four times. In a fugue, the class claps four times. While the class is clapping four times, the leader claps a new four-beat pattern such as stomping twice and clapping twice. This fugue goes on, concentrating on keeping the beat steady. When the leader is done, she folds her arms. The class finishes its four beats and then they fold their arms. The leader can also use a piano or drum to dictate the rhythms. Students will want to be the next leader, particularly if they can play the drum, so give them a chance.

Playing a mirror game yields similar results to the fugue game, but it's done with music in the background. Using any music—a movie or Broadway soundtrack, opera overture, or pop or choral music—the leader simply moves his arms, legs, and facial features. The class mirrors his movements.

6

Strengthening Your Organization: Networking and Recruiting

Acquaint yourself with key people

None of us is an island, particularly when the "us" refers to choral directors. We rely on the help and support of many people, including administrators, staff and the business community. Get to know them.

1. The Administration: Principal, Assistant Principal and Dean of Students

Often, many teachers, especially music teachers, complain that they don't get the support of the school administration. Instead of complaining, consider ways to improve the situation. Did you formally introduce yourself, and explain what your purpose is as a choral teacher and how you can be an integral part of the operation of the school as a whole? Do you have a big-picture attitude? In the midst of your frustration, consider that there's more to running a school than just facilitating your program. If you think your job is thankless, double it and that's what the administrators get for thanks. You can make your program and yourself more accessible by having an understanding of what the administrators go through in the course of a school day, much less an entire year.

If your choral program is thriving with lots of students and you are performing in and out of the school and representing the school in a positive way, the administrator will likely have the common sense to support what you are doing. This isn't to say that you will get all of the money, music or equipment you are asking for. In fact, you probably won't, but that doesn't necessarily translate to lack of support.

If you are truly not getting the support of the administration, write down all of the positives in your program and your teaching, get your ducks in a row and ask for ten minutes with the principal. Communicating your feelings may save you years of grief over something that very well could be imagined.

2. Office Manager or Secretary

The school's office manager is sometimes the most powerful person in the school, because he or she has access to everything that is happening in the school and can determine what is passed on to the administration. Office managers can decide what they will or won't relay to the principal, serving to either help or hinder your relationship with this important person. This, and many other substantial things that could make or break you and your program, will be determined by how you get along with the office manager.

Once again, having a simple understanding of the work that is piled on the office manager and approaching him or her with kindness will go much further than coming in and making belligerent demands.

3. School Counselor

There will be times when you want certain students in your program and times when you want certain students out of your program. Your rapport with the counselor—who is also the students' schedule maker at the secondary level—can very well determine whether or not a schedule will be changed to fit your choral program's request.

Counselors often feel demeaned by teachers, who treat counselors as if their job is easy because they don't have a classroom full of children to teach. Aside from being disrespectful and inappropriate, this treatment strains a relationship that is very important to the success of your choral program.

A simple thank you usually goes a long way these days. Any time counselors do anything for you or your program, be sure to thank them or buy them something they would be thrilled to have. Remember that school counselors listen to the problems of many students, parents and teachers and are expected to resolve these problems day in and day out. When their actions or decisions make someone happy, it's taken for granted. When their actions or decisions do not, the counselors hear about it over and over again. Do not fall into this trap. Be kind to your counselor, because one schedule change can help the dynamic of your entire class.

In some secondary schools, a full-time registrar is responsible for scheduling. The registrar should be met with the same care and respect as the counselor.

4. Banker

Working with money goes hand-in-hand with running a choral program. There is revenue from fundraisers and ticket sales, and expenses for contest fees and recordings, not to mention the many things for which a check needs to be cut on the spot. Establishing a respectful and competent relationship with your school's banker will make all of these transactions run more smoothly.

When some teachers have a fundraiser, they just dump the money on the banker expecting it to be counted there. Would you do this at your bank? Absolutely not! Make sure all of your deposits are carefully counted and the money is organized. If you have a huge jar of coins, take it to a place where the coins can be sorted and exchanged for paper money (provided you are authorized to do so). Not only do gestures like this go a long way towards building a good relationship with the banker, your organization will carry more weight with the banker and district auditor if there is ever a discrepancy.

5. Custodial Staff

A good relationship with the custodial staff can go a long way in supporting your choral program. While teachers and chorus students help set up for most concerts, there will come a time or two when you won't be able to. Perhaps you are teaching classes all day and there's an assembly. Perhaps you are performing during the day. It's on these occasions when the custodial staff can help with set up. A custodian is also present at school functions—from the spaghetti dinner to your winter concert to the solo and ensemble event you are hosting—and can help with things you may not even know you need. Further, the custodial staff will do a better job keeping your room neat and clean if they feel that you are appreciative of their work. This is a bridge worth building!

6. Cafeteria Staff

At first, it seems as though the school's cooking staff really has nothing to do with your choral program. This is true until you want to have a potluck or spaghetti dinner in the cafeteria and use the kitchen facilities. This is true until you want to use the cafeteria refrigerator or freezer to store your soda for a party or your cookie dough for a fundraiser. This is true until your choir is out performing and returns to school just after lunch. Wouldn't it be nice if the cafeteria workers prepared something for your students upon their return? Make sure to keep the cafeteria manager informed of how many students will be absent from lunch, and what time you would like lunch to be ready for your students.

7. Business Community

As a chorus teacher, you deal with business people all of the time. You have to work with fundraising representatives, dry cleaners, dress makers, tuxedo stores, recording engineers, video and sound technicians, engraving shops, food establishments, and so on. Remember that these people are in business to make money, not to give everything away. Just because you are a school doesn't mean that you are entitled to their services or products for free. There is an old German proverb: "Buying is cheaper than asking." Keep this in mind when you are working with businesses and think of the long-term relationship. It's normally after you've shown that you're a long-time customer who doesn't expect anything in return that the business will be more than glad to do something in kind to help you out just when you need it most.

Recruitment is key to any organization's growth and stability

In order to be an effective recruiter, you need to be armed with the support of those around you, including the students, who are perhaps the most important group of all. Your current students can be your best source of recruitment, and the way you interact with the student body as a whole is the largest determinate of your recruiting success.

Do not be too picky as you begin to build your program. Get as many students interested and involved as possible:

- Be a high-profile teacher. High-five the students in the hallway. Visit other classrooms to introduce yourself and say something about your program. Walk up and down the tables in the lunchroom and visit with the students. If you have a prep period, go to the physical education class and participate in activities with the students.

- Make posters and flyers advertising the choral program.

- Go to your feeder school and speak at an assembly or visit the classrooms. If possible, take your choir to sing. Even a few students will help personalize your program and give feeder students someone their approximate age to look up to.

- Familiarize yourself with the school's schedule so that you know how students' schedules can be adjusted to allow participation in your program.

- Call the parents of a few students who you would like to participate in your choral program.

- Ask other teachers to help publicize your choral program to their students.

- Ask your students to bring a friend to chorus auditions.

Always remember that you have the final determination over which students will join the chorus and that it's up to you to keep their interest.

Have a variety of music and learning materials ready to go—you can adjust later

When you are getting a choral program off the ground, you will want to choose music that allows the students to experience success. Don't try to teach warhorses the first couple of weeks. There is a great deal of high-quality music that is easy to teach and easy to learn. If you are still in the recruitment stage, sing music that will create feelings of "I want to be a part of that chorus!" in the students. There may even be a time when you sing a rap song. Even a rap about the presidents performed for a patriotic assembly by a chorus that isn't singing that well yet may still get several students interested in joining your choir.

Once you have the singers, you can adjust. Whether you choose music that is old or new, classical or modern, it's up to you to teach it to your students in a way that they will enjoy. If you teach well, and the students learn well and sing with a high level of musicianship, everyone involved—including your audience—will appreciate what you are doing!

Capitalize on any accomplishments

Whether you are first building your program, rebuilding a program or beginning a new year, there will always be times when it seems as though nothing is working. This can be a time of great frustration, but don't let outward frustration get in the way of progress. The choral director has a choice to help either build things up or knock things down. The choral director also has a choice to help the *students* either build things up or knock things down.

As difficult as it can seem at times, look for the good in your students and in their progress. If there is a time when your craziest student is behaving properly, let him know—tell him, write him a small note, give him an ice cream pass, tell another teacher, call his parents. When something does come together with your chorus, be outwardly ecstatic about it—the students will work that much harder the next time!

Be prepared when performing

Nothing can topple your stature as a chorus teacher or your program's reputation more than a performance that looks unorganized and unprepared. When the director looks scatter-brained or the students look dazed and confused, there can only be one person held responsible—the director.

Directors have the greatest influence on how the stage is set, how the music is prepared and how the students are guided to perform in public, not to mention how prepared they are as individuals to make it all happen in a performance. Students will dress the way you tell them to. If they are told to wear their polo shirts for that day, they will. If they told not to talk on the risers, they won't. If the music is prepared properly in rehearsals, the students will sing with confidence. If the director is prepared for all scenarios in a concert, everything will come across smoothly.

Looking and sounding your best doesn't mean that everything will go off without a hitch—that's the magic of a live performance. However, the things that are under the control of those involved should be as prepared as possible.

Make your concerts short and audience-friendly

Many chorus directors want to perform everything that was taught over the entire semester to justify their program. However, the turn off of a long concert may offset any justification of your program, as your audience may refrain from coming back to the next concert.

When it comes to speaking at a concert, stick to the program and be respectful of your audience's time. Too many times the director talks on and on about how important music is in the school, how it's undervalued, etc. While this may be true, your audience has heard it all before. Further, you are preaching to the choir. Do you remember the teacher who always gave a lecture about poor attendance and skipping class to the students who were present and had good attendance? The people in the audience are there because they support the arts, or at least they support their child in the choral program.

This doesn't mean that you can't say a few words about the selected program or offer a word of appreciation to the audience every now and then. Just choose the right time to talk; some dead time within the concert is perfect. Say what you need to say and go on with the concert. When speaking, always be careful of what you say. Often, choral directors bring politics into their comments, which will definitely turn off some of your audience members, perhaps even a close ally.

Set goals and write them down

The best way to stay focused on your goals is to think them through carefully, set some that are realistic and some that are lofty, write them down, and make a commitment to them. When you are setting your goals, have a variety of them, such as personal goals, musical goals, goals for your teaching, goals for your choral program, and goals for your students. Talk with as many people as possible to help you select, form and achieve your goals.

Turning Your Worst Critics into Your Greatest Supporters

Your most unhappy customers are your greatest source of learning.

—Bill Gates

Every program has a parent or two who believes that their child is the next musical superstar or that she never does anything wrong in your classroom or that his behavior is perfectly acceptable. Inevitably, these parents will criticize your handling of their children and ultimately make it rather difficult for you to run your program. Frustration is certainly understandable, but a better use of your time and energy is to find ways to get these parents on board with your teaching methods and even working with you. Believe it or not, you will find that some of those parents who seem totally irrational and the most dissatisfied with you will become your most loyal supporters!

When dealing with people, remember that you are not dealing with creatures of logic, but with creatures of emotion.

—Dale Carnegie

Anytime parents contact you with a concern, hear them out. As tempting as it may be to cut them off or rebut with your opinions, allow the parents to say everything they have to say. And listen carefully. If the conversation is in person, your body language should be attentive. The same goes for a telephone conversation. We've all experienced a conversation where you know the attention of the person on the other end of the call is elsewhere, be it from lack of mental focus or because they have actually begun another activity. When parents take an interest—positive or otherwise—in their child and your program, it's important. Be sure to treat it that way.

The parents' perspective will be, understandably, student-centric, but that is fine. They may calm themselves down just by having said what was on their mind, or they may solve their own problems, answer their own questions or deal with and have a solution to their own complaint. It's amazing how many times this will happen if you allow the parents to say what they have to say!

Be slow to criticize and quick to commend.

—John Wooden

Always begin your response with something positive about the child, or even the parent. As you move forward, respond directly to the points the parent made, repeating their own words if possible. They will be impressed that you paid such close attention to their comments and will approach the exchange more rationally if you address concerns in such a point-by-point manner. This is particularly true if you express your honest care and concern for the student and put your ego and desire to be "right" in the background. Hopefully, the parents' response will be, "Wow, you are a teacher who seems to know and care about my child."

Just as knowing how much you care about your students may quickly assuage their concerns, a cavalier or arrogant attitude when dealing parents will create an instant adversary. Your parents may not know a thing about choral music or teaching large classes, but that is okay. It doesn't devalue their opinion, nor does it make you superior to them. Nobody likes a know-it-all. Act like one and the parents will surely work against you.

We can do no great things—only small things with great love.

—Mother Teresa

If, after some time, the situation remains unresolved, remind the parent that your class includes many students and the needs of each individual, as well as the class as a whole, must also be taken into consideration when making decisions. Point to specifics if appropriate. Follow this explanation with, "Mrs. Smith, what would you consider a good solution to this problem?"

Oftentimes, parents will respond to such a direct question by saying that they are satisfied with your class and now understand where you are coming from as a teacher. However, you must be prepared if they offer a solution. Before the question is asked, you should have two solutions of your own in mind to use in response. You should also be prepared to honestly analyze the parents' solution. If it's satisfactory to you, offer it back to them along with one of your own solutions. Let the parent choose which is the best solution.

The time to make friends is before you need them.

—John Wooden

End just as you began—on a positive note. You may also add that you are happy to get to know the parents better and express anything that you may have learned from the conversation. Because of your efforts, even if the parents don't totally agree with the outcome, you may gain a great ally because of how reasonably you dealt with them. Sometimes, these are the same parents that will do anything they can to help you!

Showcasing Your Program: Uniforms, Recordings and Concert Deportment

Showcasing your program doesn't mean showing off yourself and your students. Rather, showcasing is a way to reach out to the community and give back to those who have helped your program. When done in the proper spirit, it's good for all involved—your students, their parents, the community, and the school and its administration—and it can pay dividends you would not have otherwise imagined.

This isn't to say that showcasing shouldn't be used as a means to validate your position or to accredit your program's stature. In actuality, *showing* others what you do is preferable to *telling* others what you do. To take advantage of this extraordinary opportunity, it's imperative for everyone involved in the program to put on the best show conceivable, both on and offstage. As the director, it's up to you to take the lead when showcasing your program, so the more you know about as many things involved with showcasing your program, the better off everyone will be!

Humility is the embarrassment you feel when you tell people how wonderful you are.

—Anon.

As their leader, you set the standard for your students and the direction of your program. It's up to you to explain to your students that once they start achieving in life, those around them will do one of two things: build them up or knock them down. Students can encourage others to build them up by remaining humble and allowing their achievements to speak for themselves. If done right, showcasing is about putting your hard work on display and letting others draw their own conclusions. If this showcasing comes with deep humility, others will tend to truly appreciate what you are showing rather than simply paying lip service to the performance. Do not feel unappreciated if you are met with this reaction; more often than not, the less people say, the deeper their appreciation.

On the other hand, a sure way to motivate others to knock you down is to act like you are "it." Be it intentional or not, if your showcase appears to be a bragging, self-promoting stunt, you *will* turn off your audience immediately and likely forever. While you may be told how wonderful your work was, there will probably be very little appreciation for it. You might also have to contend with what others say behind your back, which often creates a perception of your program that is hard to reverse.

This doesn't mean that you and your students shouldn't be proud of your work. Rather, it means that you should do the very best that you can, put it on display with humility and let others do the talking.

Think classy. Be classy.

Explain to your students that wherever they are—whether it's in your classroom, in the hallway, in other classes, in the cafeteria, at home, or out in the community—they are representing themselves, the school, their family, and your program. Moreover, they are representing their respective corps, whether it's children, adolescents, or youth in general. They should make every attempt to always carry themselves well, standing tall and always trying to uplift those around them.

Once your students embrace this philosophy, they will automatically behave in the proper way when they are representing your choral program. If they are singing for an elementary school, they will take on a leadership role. If they are singing for the elderly, they will behave with a deeper sense of appreciation to those who were born before them. If they help the destitute or homeless, they will empathize with their suffering. If they are singing for the mentally or physically challenged, they will show them greater understanding.

Uniforms

Because first impressions are often based on appearance, the clothing your choral ensembles wear is an important component of showcasing your program. In most cases, the uniform should take on the feel of the people involved, the music you are performing, and the venue you are performing in. Of course, there are always budgets to consider. Some options and their pros, cons and "watch out fors" include:

T-shirts

If you are on a very strict budget, t-shirts are a possible solution. You can have them custom silk-screened, printed or embroidered with a very simple music logo and the name of your school. Remember to keep it simple. Also, try to avoid white t-shirts if you are singing on a stage. Dark-colored shirts seem to have a more stunning effect and a more uniform look.[2]

Polo shirts

Polo shirts can be a step up from t-shirts, yet they are still relatively inexpensive. They give a very universal, standard look to a music program in any concert setting. Once again, darker colors are better. As with t-shirts, polo shirts are very low maintenance. The students can easily come to the concert dressed and ready to go. You can also have "Choir Shirt Day" at school. The students can wear their choir t-shirts or polo shirts at school all day and still look cool.

Black pants

There are two huge benefits to a uniform that includes black pants. 1) Most, if not all students, will have black pants (particularly if you permit black jeans, which, while not ideal, is a great consideration if your student's resources are limited) and 2) Black is such a universal color that it's much easier to get the entire group to "agree" on that color. If you choose,

[2] There are a number of online resources for custom T- and polo shirts, including www.schoolgarb.com

for example, dark blue pants, you will quickly discover the many interpretations of dark blue that exist in closets and stores.

Black shoes

Tell your students that they can go to a discount store and purchase black dress shoes at a very inexpensive price. All-black tennis shoes may be appropriate for a sixth grade choir, but once the students enter the seventh grade, they should be given the responsibility to buy a pair of inexpensive black dress shoes. Although black is a universal color, watch out for students who think that all black is the same as black with white stripes.

Choir robes

Many school choirs sing processionals or offer their music in reverent venues and choir robes can add a final touch. They can also create a "classical" look that complements a musical program which includes a masterwork or music from the master composers. Should your choir be invited to sing with a local arts organization in their symphony or oratorio, choir robes are also the appropriate attire.

As musically appropriate as they may sometimes be, choir robes have their drawbacks. Choir robes should be wrinkle free and pressing them before a performance takes extra time. Students arrive in their street clothes and then don robes. They must be stored at the school, and stored in such a way as to minimize wrinkles, and there must be space and time to put the robes on over regular clothes. Robes are bulky to travel with. Also, the stoles (or removable collars) need to remain in place and straight throughout a concert in spite of their tendency to move. This is particularly problematic for younger children.

In short, choir robes are great to have for even the occasional performance, but they are high-maintenance. (If you use them, though, you will certainly have more appreciation when seeing other choirs perform in them.)

Dresses

A very sharp uniform for a concert setting, there are still a few things to keep in mind when considering dresses. Girls in middle school should wear tea-length dresses (about 1 foot above the shoes, just below the knees) to keep a dapper, yet younger look. You definitely want your choir to portray itself as it is, including the age. Girls in high school have pretty much reached their adult height, so floor-length is acceptable.

There are so many different styles of dresses to consider, you'll want to get as many samples as possible. You have to consider the types of sleeves, or even sleeveless, and the fabric, whether it's washable or dry-clean only, etc. to name just two. You also need to take into consideration how the dress is put on. For example, if it has a large zipper in the back, each girl will require help when dressing. There are many catalogs displaying dresses, but what a dress looks like in a catalog on one model doesn't show exactly how it will look on over 50 girls, or next to male counterparts.

Cost is also an important consideration, as dresses are fairly expensive (between $60.00-$125.00 and up). Also, middle school children grow from month to month, so it's more difficult to have a girl buy a dress outright that can be used throughout the duration of her school time with your choral program. With this taken into consideration, you must be very careful when ordering sizes. Always order the larger size for two reasons: the first is obvious—you allow room for alterations, and the other is that many choirs include movement and it's hard for a girl to raise her hands over her head with a tight dress.

Tuxedos

For the boys, tuxedos can add a formal look to your choir and, of course, they look great next to the girls in dresses.

- *The pants*—The nice thing about tuxedo pants is that the waist is usually made for "on the spot" altering using the metal clasp. Also, the hem can be taken down as necessary.

- *The shirt*—Many different pleat patterns are available for tuxedo shirts, so order the shirts together to ensure a uniform look. Also, many tuxedo shirts come with an expandable collar button, which is more necessary for a singer than anyone else.

- *The jacket*—The sleeves of a jacket can be altered, but the jacket itself cannot, so order the larger size. The tuxedo jacket costs about as much as the pants, shirt, tie, and cummerbund combined, so you may want to consider a tuxedo uniform of everything but the jacket. This look is just as sharp and still complements the girls' dresses.

- *Accessories*—The bowtie and cummerbund can match the material of the girls' dresses or, if the boys are performing by themselves, they can have their own look and color. To save on costs, a cummerbund is not necessary if the jacket will be worn at all times. Try to stay away from cufflinks and studs; there is always a boy who loses one or more. It's also a good idea to have a few extra bowties on hand should one be lost or damaged.

Madrigal outfits

The uniforms for madrigal singers can be as varied as madrigals themselves. You can select fabric and patterns which you, students, parent helpers, or professional seamstresses or tailors can make into any type of Madrigal, Renaissance, Elizabethan, or Court of the King uniforms. You can be as creative as you want!

- *Pauper uniforms*—This can be as simple as taking old bed sheets and making cover-clothes out of them.

- *Simple "Shakespearian"*—Pullover shirts with collars and knicker-like shorts with elastic waists for the boys and similar shirts and simple skirts with elastic waists for the girls are a low-cost option for custom-made uniforms. You can add accessories such as buttonholes and leather strings for the boys, and sashes and hairpieces or flowers for the girls.

- *Elizabethan*—Ideas in this style abound but it's very easy to go overboard. This style is very elaborate and consequently very expensive, and students (and parents) can become very competitive, driving the cost of some of these costumes to over $1,000. It sounds outrageous—and it is—but it can happen, so be careful.

There are a myriad of uniform possibilities, especially for your Madrigal Singers, so be creative and get input from everyone involved!

Stage deportment

How many times do you see a choir take the stage in a lethargic manner: nobody smiling, students talking and unsure of where to stand? By the time this choir reaches the stage, they will have already lost their audience. And no matter how great they may sound, the audience is not going to pay attention to this choir. It's not a purposeful decision; rather, they subliminally do not pay attention because the choir is not earning it. Stage deportment is one of the simplest ways to showcase your program, yet it's one of the most ignored. Make a better impression—rehearse different ways to get on and off the risers.

The chorus may enter the stage from the side or the front, they may be standing or seated, they may process from the back. There may be six risers on the stage, or ten. You must plan for all variables, whether you are familiar with that stage or not. Your audience will not know, or care.

Get the "end students" of each side of the risers into the habit of standing a certain space toward the edge and have the choir fill in accordingly. Too often when choirs are taking the stage, the students "bunch up" on one side and the director has to spread them out. This always gets an uncomfortable audience response, and the choir loses its energy before singing one note. Even if you are used to singing on six risers, spreading out on eight or even ten risers means that there will be only a little more space between each singer. This actually can make for a better look, and a better sound!

Unless you have the perfect situation to line up the students and take the risers one row at a time, have the students find their spot on the risers, and take it immediately. If you line up in rows, the choir is often lined up backwards depending on where you were sitting, or after finding out that you are taking the stage from the opposite side. This can all be avoided, and you can cut down on a great deal of time, when you train your students to just "take their spot" on the risers. Even if the director has to re-space the choir, it looks a lot less awkward than if the choir is bunched together.

If your concerts are in the school gymnasium, you can have the students sit on the floor (with the audience on the bleachers) in the order that each chorus is going to sing. After one chorus is through singing, they can part in the middle, go off the sides, sit in the back of the chorus students who are on the floor. While that is happening, the next choir runs up and takes their space on the risers. This should take no more than 30 seconds! Think of the time you are saving! If you do it "cattle call" style, you will be surprised of how attentive your audience will be, not only because of how quickly and organized the students took the stage, but also because you saved them five minutes between each choir and a half hour over the entire concert!

Train your students to never talk on the risers. Most of the time, the talking students are just trying to "help" other students take their places. However, if the director properly trains the students, there is no need for this. Tell your students that if any adjustments are necessary, they will be done only by the director.

Many singers want to know what to do with their hands. Train your students to put their fingertips on the sides of their pants, and keep them there until they are completely off the stage. Basically, once the chorus is on the stage, their hands never leave the sides of their pants. If they have an itch, tell them that it will eventually go away. Tell the girls with long hair to put it in a barrette so that they do not flick their hair. Whenever anyone is in full-concentration mode, the mind tells the body to not sneeze or cough, so concentrate and this will not be a problem!

Your students should stand on the risers with their feet underneath the shoulders for the best possible support. It's impractical for each chorus student to stand with one foot in front of the other. This is fine for one singer, but not the chorus as a whole. One reason why singers are told to put one foot in front of the other is so that the knees do not lock. The blood flow will not be hindered if the student is standing up straight. It will only be hindered if the student squeezes or "locks" his knees.

Just as important as stage deportment while the chorus students are singing on the stage is how well the chorus students are behaving when the other choirs are singing. Train your students that when they are in the audience, they are still performing. Tell them to never talk in the audience while other choirs are singing. Most of the time, they are making nice comments to their friends about what they are seeing and hearing, but the students need to know that this is still distracting to the chorus on the stage because they do not know what you are talking about!

Pictures

Photographs of the choir offer endless showcasing possibilities:

- You can frame the pictures and hang them in your room for all to see—future students, parents, administrators, faculty and staff, members of the community and most of all, your chorus alumni. The memories of their time in your program will become more cherished as the years go on and they will appreciate having been captured for posterity.
- You can also use the pictures on programs and promotional posters, the cover of your albums or in a portfolio.
- The photos can become the centerpiece of a plaque thanking area businesses for their support or honoring dignitaries for whom you sang. The group photo can also be used on any choir awards.
- Selling picture packages can be a profitable fundraiser, as well as a thoughtful and meaningful way to involve all students and their families in fundraising efforts.

Should you decide to have pictures taken of the choir, you first need to secure a professional photographer. His or her fees are an important consideration, as are the package options for students. A typical package offering is as follows:

Package A:	Three 8x10 group photos	$20.00
Package B:	Three 5x7 group photos	$15.00
Package C:	Three 8x10 group photos and individual package*	$30.00
	+ Eight wallets	$35.00
Package D:	Three 5x7 group photos and individual package	$25.00
	+ Eight wallets	$30.00

* Four 3x5 photos and eight wallets.

Once a photographer and photo package are in place, you need to plan the photo shoot. Make it an important day for students! Of course, you always have the option of having picture day at your concert, and if you are on location, this may be an ideal opportunity. However, if you can have a designated day where the students get into their concert attire in a controlled setting for the sole purpose of a photo shoot, the pictures will be that much nicer.

The possibilities for poses and locations are endless, so be sure to have an idea of what you want before picture day. You may want a pose on the choral risers and a pose without the risers. You may choose a pose indoors and a pose outdoors. Remember that weather has a way of not cooperating, so always have a plan B. A day devoted to pictures with all of your choirs is stressful enough without the complications of Mother Nature.

If you are traveling and want a special remembrance of a tour or performance, you can go online and find a professional photographer to meet you at the concert or a specific location. Agree to the terms, packages, location, and poses in writing and prior to your arrival. It's also wise to ask those coordinating the event for permission to take photographs. In some prominent or historical venue, such as Washington National Cathedral in Washington, D. C., Orchestra Hall in Chicago, or Carnegie Hall in New York, it's required. In all instances, though, these people are usually very cooperative and may offer a box seat to your photographer so he or she can take the best possible photo.

Once you have your professional photographs, take them to a professional frame shop to add the final touch. This picture is an important, permanent remembrance for many different people to see for a very long time to come. Do not be afraid to spend a little extra money for a stunning finished product!

Audio recording

In recent years, the costs to produce a CD recording have fallen so much that almost every program is able to afford one and reap the many benefits. Like chorus photos, a recording of your ensemble is a powerful showcasing tool within the school and community and is helpful when securing future performing opportunities. It's a lifetime keepsake for everyone involved with the program and can be the keystone of a successful fundraising effort.

There are four steps to most recording projects:

1. Securing mechanical licenses
2. Recording and post-production
3. Packaging
4. Duplicating

1. Securing mechanical licenses

Just as you must secure permission and sometimes pay a fee to make photocopies of a copyrighted work, you must secure permission and pay any fees—called mechanicals—before recording any copyrighted pieces of music. Every copyright holder handles requests differently, but most take two to four weeks to process licenses. Typical questions you should be prepared to answer include how many CDs you are duplicating and how much you are charging for the CD.[3]

2. Recording and post-production

There are several options when recording: you can record live at a concert; you can record on location; or you can go to a studio, if they have facilities for a large group. The record-

[3] See Appendix B for publisher contact information.

ing method and the amount of time spent in post-production affect the cost.

a. *Recording live at a concert with no post-production.* This is the easiest option when recording. You simply call a recording engineer who will set up and record at your concert. Most engineers can give you a master CD recording on the spot at the end of the concert. That easy, and *wow!*, you have a CD of your choir. You simply duplicate your CDs from this master.

b. *Recording live at a concert with post-production.* The process begins as above—a recording engineer comes to your concert and gives you a CD on the spot—but instead of duplicating from this CD, you take it to a recording engineer for post-production (it's a good idea to use the same engineer who recorded the concert). In post-production, the recording will be manipulated with a software program. Background noise can often be removed, as can dead time between pieces. Each piece from the concert will also be given its own track, which is a very professional touch. One note: since it's a live recording, including the applause at the end of each piece with a fade to the end of the track is recommended.

c. *Recording on location with post-production.* "On location" can be as simple as your choir room or a local church, or it can be a recording studio. There are several advantages to recording on location, but the greatest is that you have control over what is recorded. There is no audience noise, no babies crying, nor any unexpected sounds. That is not to say that the conditions will be perfect. If you record in your choir room or a church, be careful of air coming from a vent. Whether it's heat or air conditioning, any airflow can really muffle the sound of your choir. You can control this by placing someone in charge of turning off the air just before you record and turning it on during non-recording times. Another benefit of recording on location—you can begin a piece again, regardless of the reason. Once you have a recording you are satisfied with, you can take it into post-production and work with your engineer to create the best CD possible.

3. Packaging

CD packaging can range from a simple label available at most office-supply stores that you can ink-jet or laser print to a full-color design printed on the CD with matching glossy tray card and insert. Although packaging can quickly become more expensive than the recording and post-production costs combined, attractive and professional options exist throughout this spectrum.

A very affordable option, the simple, do-it-yourself label is often sufficient because it shows through the case. You can also have the label printed directly on the CD. This creates a sharper label and you can likely find an option in your budget, particularly if you are willing to minimize the number of colors in your design.

Another option is to have a cover insert and tray card (which you see on the back of the case) printed professionally. Costs vary based on the number of pages in the insert and the number of colors in your design. However, if you are already going to the expense of these elements, it's nice to use more than one color. Using a full-color image, such as a photo of the choir, can be very expensive but regardless of the cost, remember that the cover is the first thing people are going to see. It may not matter if it's just for choir students, but if you want to extend your sales to a broader market, a very professional-looking label, cover and back can make or break a sale.

4. Duplicating

There are two ways to duplicate CDs—pressing and burning. Pressing stamps the recorded information into a material similar to tin foil, which is then affixed to a plastic disc. Burning uses a laser to transfer the recorded information to an assembled but blank CD. Believe it or not, burning 100 CDs can cost as much as pressing 1000 CDs. If you want your CDs right now, your engineer can burn them a few at a time until you have as many as you want. If you can wait a few weeks, you can order from a company who duplicates CDs as well as covers and labels in bulk.

Certainly, you have to decide what is best for you, but if you are going to pay for 100 CDs, you may as well have 1000 CDs for the same cost. This way, you always have CDs on hand to send to anyone interested in your program. Also, they are nice to have when you are traveling. (Professional CD duplicators abound and their prices for duplication and printing vary greatly. A little time spent researching them can lead to a great deal of savings.)

Always give your very best effort to make the best recording and packaging possible. It's well worth the extra expense in the long run. After all, ours is an aural art. You do not want to "showcase" your choir with a shabby-sounding product.

Video recording

Making a video recording of your choir presents the same benefits as an audio recording and requires the same decisions, except that you have to wear your concert attire when recording your "music video."

There are a few technical differences between the two:

- You have the option to record the sound live when making the video, or you can dub the audio from your CD recording over the video.
- There are two video formats—VHS tapes and DVDs. The costs to produce a DVD have dropped dramatically recently, so much so that it's worth exploring the medium. You can even burn them from your own computer these days.

Once you have your video recordings—whether made on location or while traveling—you can go to a video recording studio and create a video sample of your choir. This can be used not only to showcase your program, but also for recruitment to other students and your feeder schools.

The right music for every setting

No matter how well prepared your choirs are musically, there are several things you need to keep in mind for an outstanding performance. Among these is choosing the right music—the right music for your choir and the right music for a given concert setting and audience.

Although your specialty as a musician or director may be a specific type or style of music, you don't want to fall into the trap of doing this music over and over. Nor should you cave to programming only the style of music your students like. You must always challenge yourself to expose your students to many different genres of music. Further, you must keep your repertoire updated with the many new compositions being offered each year.

Knowing your audience and knowing how and, especially, when to "educate" that audience without turning them off is another important skill of repertoire selection. For instance, if you are singing at an elementary school, either as a concert or for recruiting, there is nothing wrong with singing perhaps one classical piece of music, but do not overload the performance with the same style of music. Instead, you may be performing music that was very easy to learn and very simple to sing, but most importantly, it was also very enjoyable for your audience.

Planning your performances for the entire year and learning as much diverse music as possible is another good tip. There may be occasions when you need to unveil a new piece before it's perfect, and that's okay. You don't need to explain to the audience that this is a work in progress, unless it's within the context and flow of your program. If it's appropriate, you can say something like, "We're really excited to sing this next number for you, even though we're still working on it. And even though it's not perfect yet, please remember to clap when we're finished singing it!"

Find the right accompanist

The hours and hours spent rehearsing the chorus for a performance can turn on your choice of an accompanist. Although the director may be the best accompanist for some situations, for most concert settings it looks and sounds more professional to use an accompanist. And as any director knows, an outstanding piano player doesn't necessarily make a great accompanist.

Find an accompanist who will be sensitive to the demands of the music and, if possible, one who has experience singing in a choir. You should find an accompanist who will work well with you and the students. It can be a sick feeling for everyone involved to see a director and accompanist fighting with each other over the music. Remember that the accompanist (unless with you from the start) doesn't know the musical nuances as well as you, or even your students. It's up to you as the director and musical leader to help the accompanist be a fine addition to the choral music.

Awards banquet

Having an awards banquet is a great way for everyone to come together in a good-natured, social setting. You can invite alumni, have guest speakers and perform a few numbers.

Bring kids on stage

Inviting brothers, sisters and other young kids from the audience onstage to sing a song with your choir touches everyone. Create this opportunity by adding a simple song like "Rudolf the Red-Nosed Reindeer" or "Jingle Bells" to the end of your program.

9 Festivals, Contests and Guest Conductors

Part 1: Being Judged Without Feeling Judged

After spending many hours gathering music, recruiting singers, managing many different personalities, preparing uniforms and staging—to name just a few choir-director duties—it's only natural to want to present your choral program at its best because it's a reflection of your work. Further, when you are in a festival setting, an atmosphere of competitiveness can occur. Who would want their choral program to appear and sound inferior when compared to the preceding or following choir? To make matters worse, the festival may post the results to the public, award a championship trophy or rank or place your choir relative to others.

The moment of victory is much too short to live for that and nothing else.

—Martina Navratilova

Competition can help motivate anyone and, in many cases, it's good for everyone involved. However, it's up to the director to keep things in the proper perspective. If the main focus of your festival is beating the other choir or getting a superior rating, you will most definitely be disappointed with the outcome, regardless of what it is. If you do achieve a superior rating or win first place, it's a short-term feeling of success. You get exactly what you focused on, but now that you have that rating or that trophy, what else is left? If you focus on the music—on everything it takes to make it as beautiful as possible, on sharing your music and the joy of singing with the audience—everyone will get a feeling of fulfillment. And unlike audience response and the adjudication and final marks of the judges, these elements are totally under your control.

Many directors are faced with administrators who base their evaluation of your job performance on the choir's rating. You must talk with them and share your philosophy that the festival and its ratings are only a part of your overall educational philosophy when directing your choral program. You cannot expect the administrators to fully understand everything that your job involves, but if you explain things in a prudent manner, your administrators will most likely understand. On the other hand, if you don't keep your administrators informed, know that they will most likely base their feelings about or evaluation of the program on your rating because they will have nothing else to base it upon.

Success is a journey, not a destination.

—Anon.

The director must make it clear to his or her students that the judges sincerely do the best job that they can to give constructive criticism while adjudicating, but in the end, the judges must select a winner or give an overall rating. Even if it's not the rating you would have expected or what you would have liked, use it as a learning experience and always focus on the positives.

If you have the opportunity to plan a choral festival or make suggestions about one already in place, do everything you can to make it what it is—a festival! Focus the students on being cordial toward other choir students. Use it as a venue for them to meet new people, exchange ideas about chorus, and promote their overall educational and personal experience. Choirs should have the opportunity to listen to each other, and cheer for one another. If your choir has seen and heard other groups, you will have the opportunity to point out positives and negatives when teaching. You will also be able to better explain the results of other choirs as compared to your own, be they better or worse. Cheering for each other fosters a collegial spirit, but know that to feel comfortable cheering, students need to know that their directors (and all adults involved with the program) are cheering for everyone as well. Believe it or not, the students will take a poor showing (or even a failure to come in first) much *better* than you, provided you are like most directors—your own worst critic. If you feel badly about your rating or placement, get over it and move on!

Practical pointers

Do not focus your entire year's literature on the pieces you are performing at the festival. This is a sure way to get caught in the over-learning trap, causing the music to become stale. Rather, select your music to complement your entire year.

Notes to the judges should be about the music, and only the music. Mark any changes (cuts, doubling of parts, changing of parts, etc.) in the judges' copies. Include a road map of your music if you need to. Do not write a personal note to the judges about your choir. Do not say, "this is a low-achieving group"; "we just started this music last week due to..."; "this is a non-auditioned group"; "we are missing our two best basses"; "we are a low-income school because..."; "many of our students cannot afford uniforms..." Just *don't* do it.

Prepare your students for anything. You may have to change venues, times or rooms. You may have to sing for a different set of judges. Everyone has to be flexible in a festival setting.

Finally, don't rip your hair out when planning for a festival. Just keep things in perspective and things will have a way of working out.

Part 2: Preparing Your Program and Your Students for a Guest Conductor

Linda Spevacek

A successful festival or all-state choir is one of the most exhilarating events a participating student and his or her director can experience. Singing with a large group offers new perspectives on the school's own choir and its singers. It brings awareness of new literature. Directors are motivated to bring this opportunity to students and themselves and engage in healthy competition in search of excellence. Students learn about self-discipline in relation to the group dynamics.

Unfortunately, none of these benefits make planning a festival or all-state choir any easier. Bringing a group of students unfamiliar with each other together and putting a new face in front of them is difficult. Here are some suggestions to help make your event run more smoothly:

Keep a journal of the process...and share it! Don't start over every year. Get in the habit of writing down what goes right, what goes wrong, what you should have done differently, who should be assigned to what, and the like. Make dividers for each section. Each year, pass on these journal sections to the new person in charge and suggest that he or she update the journal. Why start out as a novice if you don't have to?

Send or fax the conductor programs from the past 3-5 years. Previous programs give the conductor an idea of the general skill level of the student pool along with the balance of musical elements, including musical style (classical works, spirituals, etc.) and instrumentation.

Send any state requirements and standards to the guest conductor before he or she spends time choosing a program.

Instruct the local directors to attend all rehearsals. The presence of their directors will tell students—and the guest conductor—that this festival is important. The directors may also learn new techniques in the process, but more importantly, they'll understand what the students experienced and can help lead a follow up discussion when back in class. Director attendance also avoids any potential, "If it's time for the teachers to take a break from school, why not us too?" attitude from students.

Discipline should be handled by the local director, not by the guest conductor. Singing in a large festival choir is a new situation for many students and maintaining order can be a challenge. The local directors can be of immense help. Students face their own director in school the following school day, not the guest conductor. And while it may not be necessary, individual directors have the power to affect grades, notify parents, issue detentions, etc.

Establish an atmosphere of excellence beforehand. Introduce behavior expectations—in writing—prior to the festival and distribute them to participating students and parents. Once the festival has begun, stick to the rules. This includes consequences if the rules are not followed. Students, particularly the top singers, will not repeat a festival that tolerates behavior distractions and will set their own standards if given the opportunity. Ask them what behaviors they won't accept and what they feel the penalties should be.

Insist that all students have the music committed to memory. If students have spent enough time to memorize the music it means they have spent time with the music. In addition to giving individuals self-confidence in their singing, the sound of the choir is going to be better from the get-go, setting up a positive group experience right out of the gate. That time doesn't have to be spent on "notes" and that attention will be on the conductor and not shuffling music, which goes a long way to an outstanding final performance. A group who's memorized their parts also sends a positive message to the guest conductor about your festival's effective audition process and overall commitment to quality.

Have students mark the measure numbers in every piece before the first rehearsal. Even when music is memorized, it's important to work out details with the music. Having the measure numbers marked allows for quick referral to the corrections needed whereas counting and finding measures wastes precious time that could be utilized singing and perfecting the music.

Instruct students to bring two sharpened or mechanical pencils to the festival or all-state site. It's also a good idea for directors to bring sharpened, backup pencils.

Give the guest conductor the name and contact numbers of the person responsible for the airport pickup (a mobile number, if available, is particularly helpful). Many times a person other than the initial contact handles the transportation. When a plane is late or the driver is caught in traffic, there can be total confusion. The less energy clinicians have to exert while traveling, the more energy they save for the rehearsal.

Be prepared to pay the fee and expenses at the end of the last day. Check approximate expenses with the conductor up front. If he or she has a contract, make sure it's signed at the same time as the festival's contract. Oftentimes, details in his or her contract can answer many of your questions. Run a festival like you would run a business. Reimburse fees and expenses in a timely manner. Never put a conductor in the position of having to call repeatedly to collect unpaid sums. Efficient handling of these matters will result in kudos from your conductor about your well-run festival that allows for an all-around, wonderful musical experience for all, and they will share the kudos with other conductors you may hope to invite to your festival.

Part Three

A Music Teacher is a Musician

10 Voice Lessons in the Choral Classroom

Teaching a chorus to sing with proper vocal techniques is very similar to a private teacher giving voice lessons to a single student, so treat it that way. Adopt a "one on one" mentality and engage every member of the chorus in this way. Teach concepts and exercises the same way a private teacher would.

Breathing

Proper breathing techniques and exercises are something that can be worked on every day, even if it's for a few minutes. Breathing exercises can begin with a long exhale. When the lungs are empty, they will fill efficiently and in the proper place. You can instruct the singers to blow air into their fists or "blow out candles" on their finger with shallow breaths, followed by a long inhale. Always remind the singers that whenever they breath in, it *must* be an inaudible, relaxed inhale (similar to a slight yawn). Once you have taught your breathing techniques, remind the chorus students to breathe often—it will prevent many potential problems and help make a beautiful tone with long, musical phrases. Deep breathing will also prevent vocal fatigue.

"Support it from the diaphragm" is a commonly heard phrase when it comes to breathing. In actuality, the diaphragm controls the breath, not necessarily supports it. The choir students should learn that the support begins with a firm, yet comfortable, foot position, strong trunk of the body, and tall, yet relaxed, upper body. When the students feel the whole body as part of supporting the breath and vocal sound, they will produce more depth in their singing. Once this is achieved, the concept of the diaphragm controlling the breath can be more attainable, which, in turn, produces a full sound and arched phrase.

Posture

One way to establish a body ready to sing is to have the students inhale while raising their hands over their heads and exhale as they reach to touch their toes. The students can stay down for a short period of time and relax their breathing back to a natural state. Then, the students should be instructed to "stack the vertebrae." Have them stand up very, very slowly beginning with their tailbone, feeling the bottom of the spine—vertebra by vertebra—stack all the way up to the base of the neck and eventually to the base of the skull. This technique works wonders to develop great posture.

When it's not one-on-one

While you should approach the teaching of these skills as a private teacher, you are still in front of a class, which presents its own unique demands. When it comes to holding interest, a large group is very different from a private one-on-one lesson. Make your vocal techniques meaningful to the context of the music, developing the voice and building a beautiful choral tone. Never overkill a technique. You can always come back to it as the situation arises.

Know that teaching vocal techniques can sometimes create an awkward or potentially silly situation, particularly because of the dynamic in a large group. It's very important for you to be matter of fact when the students are practicing vocal techniques to avoid silly reactions from the class. Don't talk your way into a silly situation. Simply teach what you want your students to learn and leave it at that.

From my perspective...
by Linda Spevacek

Posture

- Use a winner's philosophy stance. Say and think, "I am a winner," and stand accordingly.

Breath Support

- Avoid using the phrase, "Sing with your diaphragm." The diaphragm is an involuntary muscle and has a mind of its own. It goes in and up towards the spine all by itself, without any direct control from the singer. Don't try to sing and manipulate the diaphragm; it can cause unneeded tension in the throat.

- The singer must expand the ribcage, fill the lungs, learn to take low breaths and make good use of the abdominal muscles. Then the diaphragm is able to do what it does best naturally.

Tone

- The beauty of singing is on the vowel. Students must spend time on all ten vowels in the low, middle and high part of the range, making them consistent in function and thus consistent in sound.

Diction

- The drama of music is in the consonant. We must learn to exaggerate the consonants on the words we want to stress in the phrase. Listen to musical theater performers for good examples. The story is key and so it should be with choirs, no matter what the language, style, mood or tempo.

The Face Factor

Imago animi vultus est indices oculi. *(The countenance is the portrait of the mind; the eyes are its informers.)*

—Cicero

- 55% of all communication is body language, 38% is the tone used and only 7% is in the words spoken (or sung). In choral singing, singers must look involved in their music. Make sure the audience can *hear* their faces.

- Tell your students that they are entertainers...each one of them. Teach them to cross the footlights, reach out and grab the audience, tug at their heartstrings, get the audience involved in our music.

- Ask to feel, emote, to get out of themselves and into the text and the music, to come alive, be on fire, sing with passion.

11 Working with the Boy's Voice

Whether you are dealing with the unchanged, changing, adolescent, or young man's voice, gaining as much knowledge as you possibly can is key to a successful choral program. Becoming aware of the advantages and disadvantages inadvertently created by your own gender can enhance this knowledge. Hence the unique approach of two independent perspectives: one from a male teacher, one from a female. The goal is for a teacher of either gender to be able to take both of these perspectives and use them to help work with the boy's voice.

Part 1: From a Male Teacher's Perspective

Adolescence is a time when students not only have to deal with the changing voice but also with great emotional stress. This is especially true for the adolescent boy. Many chorus teachers will say that dealing with the boy's changing voice is their single most important task and greatest challenge when teaching middle school chorus. Consequently, it's a subject of much expert research and frequent discussion. Although these more academic approaches serve an important purpose, it's the intent of this chapter to share less-formal tips and techniques that have been, and continue to be, effective when working with the boy's voice.

Open a class exclusively for the boys

Do whatever it takes to open a section for your sixth-grade class that is open to boys only.

Start by saying "Zing!" Singing begins with an "A"

Begin by having the boys say "Zing!" Repeat until it's said with the energy you require. Then have the boys sing in unison, "Zing, zing, zing, zing, zing" [1, 2, 3, 2, 1], beginning on A below middle C. (Too many teachers begin with middle C. Boys want to jump down the octave when singing middle C, which will lose them quickly and surely.)

Get your boys to do the siren sound to get acclimated with and to develop their head voice

Many times, boys will sing an octave or even a perfect fourth or fifth below the given note or melody because they think, "boys sing low." You can quickly solve this by having the boys sing a "siren" sound (a police officer driving a patrol car is an impressive and masculine description for a boy). You can also have the boys do the "You! You! You!" sound that's made at a basketball game when the opposition makes a foul, with their fists pounding in a circular motion above their heads. Finally, you can tell the boys that you are on a roller coaster ride: their hands imitate the ride; the voice goes low when the coaster is down and high when the coaster is at the top.

A boy has a small range only when speaking

When students begin singing seriously, their point of reference is their speaking voice and boys usually speak with less inflection than girls. As a result, when they begin singing boys don't know where the other areas in their voices "feel," much less how to match a musical pitch. As the boys become more comfortable singing and matching pitches, their range will increase accordingly.

Divide your boy's choir into three parts

Return to the "zing" exercise, moving up by half steps until the boys are singing a D or E above middle C. When finished, ask the boys who could sing those notes to raise their hands. Many will raise their hands but it's important to listen to each individually. If a boy is able to do it with ease, tell him to move to the right third of the class because he is in "Part 1." Do *not* say "soprano" or "high part," as it may work to everyone's disadvantage, especially yours! Use Part 1 instead, which will give the boys the feeling of "We're Number One!" Continue this process until about one-third of the boys are in Part 1.

Have the remaining students sing the same vocal exercise, this time moving down by half steps. Listen for the boys who can sing an F below middle C comfortably. These boys will stand in the middle third of the choir and are Part 3. Continue this vocal exercise until all boys who are able to sing the F below middle C can do so comfortably; usually this will be a bit less than one third of the choir. The remaining boys are obviously Part 2.

This process should take less than ten minutes. Once the boys are in their respective sections, continue with the same vocalization. Each and every boy will sing with a full, secure voice. Do not stretch the exercises up or down too far; make sure the boys retain a unison and none of them drop down the octave.

Move any true bass into your SATB choir

If there is a boy or two who truly sings bass, which is not all that unusual in the sixth grade, place that boy in your SATB chorus, no matter if it's a seventh- or eighth-grade chorus. Explain to your counselor or administrator why this is absolutely necessary. They will honor your request if you're running a successful program and come across as if you know what you are talking about. If this placement is not possible, it's not the end of the world; just place these boys in Part 3.

Boys and girls in the same class need organization

If, for school scheduling reasons, it isn't possible to have an All-Boys Choir, then you need to find ways to work with both sixth-grade boys and sixth-grade girls in the same class. Although this isn't the first choice, it's workable if you know how to organize it.

Begin with the same "zing" vocalization, but this time you are working to divide the girls into Part 1 and Part 2. All of the boys will sing Part 3.[4] In this situation, you can call Part 1 the "sopranos," Part 2 the "altos," and Part 3 the "tenors," because all of the boys are "tenors." Regardless of the gender of your middle school choir members, your goal should be to place students in their respective sections quickly and efficiently. The main objective in the beginning choirs is to spark an interest and have the students experience success quickly and often. Taking days or weeks to voice test the students one-by-one at the piano is a sure way to ensure that the rest of your year will be spent on classroom-management damage control. Remember, you can always move singers while you are rehearsing if you feel that they would be more comfortable singing in a different section.

Although some notes in Part 3, like G or F, may be a little low for some boys, instruct those boys to sing in a light tone or not at all. Instruct them to "open your mouth to where it feels the note is, but do not actually sing it" and to "wait to sing until you are in a more comfortable range." Always keep in mind that one objective is to develop your choirs. Most sixth-grade boys will be able to sing all of Part 3 by the end of the year and then these boys will be ready for your three-part seventh-grade choir, or the SATB eighth-grade choir.

Another important objective to remember—keep your students interested and enthused about singing in choir. If boys

---

[4] There are choral educators who don't feel that boys capable of singing soprano and/or alto should automatically be assigned to Part 3 in a boy/girl choir. If it works for you to have the boys sing in these respective sections without any social repercussions, and without affecting the interest level of the boys in the current year and for years to come—go for it! As always, use the method that works best for you and your students.

are told to sing the same part as the girls, you may immediately lose their interest, and never regain it.

You got the boys...now get them singing!

In the sixth-grade chorus with all boys, teach the boys singable folk songs or patriotic songs in unison. Have the boys echo back one phrase at a time and before you know it, they will be singing *with you* for the next line because they are extremely enthused by your rehearsal and are instinctively singing the music. Children love to sing! Adolescents love to sing! People love to sing! It's only natural. Capitalize on this.

Unison songs that all the boys can sing include: "Buffalo Gals," "Clementine," "*Du, du, liegst mir im Herzen*," "Skip to My Lou," "Sun Magic," "La Bamba," "Donna," and "Old Time Religion."

Know your stuff on the piano while teaching the boys

When teaching all boys, you must have the songs you're teaching down cold and be very secure with your playing on the piano. You must be able to keep eye contact with the boys while you are playing, because they will get really squirrelly, and you will lose them fast!

You must also be able to transpose at will when teaching boys. This is not as difficult as it sounds because most folk and patriotic songs follow a three-chord progression, but you must practice until you can do it easily.

Yes, practicing the piano enough to become proficient at both of these skills will take a little extra time, but it will be repaid to you tenfold by the classroom-management time you've saved that can now be spent on choral rehearsal and music education.

Teach them three-part music the first day

Now that the boys have sung unison songs successfully, you can teach them three-part music very easily.

For example, consider the popular, "The Lion Sleeps Tonight," or any other recognizable song with three distinct melodies. Instruct Part 3 to stand and teach them their part; repeat for Parts 2 and 1. Now have Part 3 join Part 1; have Part 2 sing along. Now have Part 2 and Part 3 sing together. Ask for Part 1 and Part 2 to sing. Just jump in and say, "Parts 1 and 3—let's go!" Do *not* waste time talking and explaining! There shouldn't be dead time or talking time in between—just singing.

The minute you stop the process to give your intellectual, analytical thoughts, learning stops taking place. If the boys don't sing exactly the way you would like them to at this particular time, it's okay! Remember—you have the rest of the year. In the beginning, your objective is to get them turned on to your choral program and keep their interest. Once this occurs, the rest will fall into place.

Get those boys up and moving with choralography

Boys at this age love to move! Use it to your advantage to hold their interest and channel their energy in a positive way. When teaching boys simple choralography, never make a big deal about it...just do it! If you give a long explanation of why you are doing something, you muddy the activity and allow time for apprehension to creep in. (The thinking here is similar to not verbalizing or reinforcing negative behavior.)

Tips to get the boys to sing on pitch

Imagine teaching a child with two different legs and two different arms to ride a bicycle. That is what it's like teaching a boy who is going through his voice change to sing on pitch. Not only is a singer asked to hear a pitch, he's asked to sing it back as well. He has to internalize the pitch that he hears, which may be different from the one you hear, and sing it back with his vocal apparatus, which feels completely different from the one he has been familiar with for years and years. Talk about difficult![5] Like riding a bike, learning to sing on pitch can be very frustrating at first, but once the child has the hang of it, he will have the hang of it for life!

---

[5] Do not explain these physiological factors to the boy—it will only make things worse.

1. Keep in mind that what you hear is not necessarily what the boy hears. If you hear a pitch on the piano, the boy may hear a certain overtone instead of the fundamental. Give the boy different examples: playing in octaves or an octave above; use another student as an example, whether a boy on the same pitch, or a girl an octave higher. Allow the boy to experiment. Eventually, he will be able to match the pitch using his voice in a trial-and-error approach.

2. If a boy is singing off pitch, sing the same pitch back to him and slide up or down (usually up, since the boys tends to sing below the pitch) until the boy hears and sings the correct pitch. Repeat as necessary. Even when the boy begins below the pitch, he will sometimes start higher than that pitch on the second or third attempt. This is only natural. You must stick to it until they eventually get the correct pitch.

3. Sometimes, just as it is with other areas of learning—especially physical learning—success usually begins with the offering of encouragement. If a boy begins below the given pitch, say very enthusiastically, "That's close, but you need to sing it higher. Come on, you can do it!" If the boy sings the exact same pitch the exact same wrong way, repeat your verbal encouragement. (More commonly, the boy will sing the exact same pitch but louder, thinking it's higher.) Don't use any negative verbiage when trying to get the boy to sing on pitch. Instead, focus on singing the correct pitch. Always stay positive and be encouraging. Eventually, the boy will sing on pitch!

4. Along with the verbal encouragement, take your fist up to the boy's stomach and "wind him up" like an organ grinder. The boy will have a tendency to slide up to the correct pitch, and when he does, let him know it right away. Have him sing the pitch back again. If necessary, repeat this process until the boy is able to sing the correct pitch consistently.

The second the boy sings on pitch, give him a big verbal and physical gesture to let him know that he zeroed in on the pitch. Have him sing it again. Even if he's off pitch this time, chances are that the pitch is closer *and* that the boy will be able to adjust to the correct pitch much more easily than the first time. Keep it up and keep encouraging him. Eventually, he will "feel" where the pitch is in his vocal apparatus and be better able to "hear" where the pitch is. Indeed, taking the time to get your boys to sing on pitch is a small investment that pays huge dividends!

Keep the boys on pitch by quizzing them nonchalantly

Throughout a rehearsal, or at any time during the class—when taking attendance or when there's a hall runner coming to the class for an errand, for example—have the boy match and sing a random pitch. When matching pitch quickly and spontaneously, the boy doesn't have time to clench his throat or mind and will likely find success. When he does, give him an energetic, positive response in front of the whole class. Pretty soon, he will match pitches consistently, become more and more comfortable with his voice, and be able to sing just as beautifully as you teach him to sing—not only by himself, but also with the whole choral ensemble. And with this voice lesson completed, you can resume your role as the choral director to make the boy an integral part of the chorus.

Guide the boys through their grade transitions

Most boys, particularly those that began choir with you in the sixth grade, will make the transition from soprano or alto to tenor or bass rather easily. Keep track of their register progress. Every so often, simply write down their lowest note and see how full they can sing it. This will help you determine where their voice is going.

While you should do the same for those tenors and basses who tend to sing off pitch, you must also teach them to sing on pitch consistently. Oftentimes, these are students with no previous choral experience who have joined your choir in the eighth grade, so you may need to modify exercises you used with their classmates when they were in the earlier grades. It can be frustrating at first, but it's well worth the time and energy once the boy sings on pitch consistently. Who knows, he may be on his way to becoming a star bass!

The best model of the voice is the director singing in a light tone

Often, a young male singer will strain his voice to try to compete with the volume, sonority and timbre of the female voice. This is the equivalent of a trombone trying to compete with the musical sound of a piccolo. It's not going to happen. Each instrument has its own unique quality, and the same is true for the unique differences between the male and the female voice. Whether you are a male or female instructor of the voice, it's always necessary to model in a light tone to develop the best tone quality.

Boys need more attention and encouragement in chorus

If a boy takes the initiative to join your chorus, you can be certain that there were one or more hurdles for him to jump over: giving up another interesting class; overcoming any social ramifications; battling fears that he's not a good singer; or feeling dissatisfied with his voice or even very shy using it. While you should not be afraid to have the boy sing in the class and correct his voice as necessary, be sure he knows that you are doing this for his benefit and not to embarrass him. Keep in mind all he went through to join your choir and make sure that you encourage him along the way.

Part 2: From a Female Teacher's Perspective

First and foremost, any male of any age needs to feel you are genuinely excited about working with his voice. Let him know that you've always had wonderful luck teaching males. There can be a stigma attached to a male who studies with a female teacher. Some parents, family and even voice teachers feel that a male must study with a male. One of the biggest differences in success is how the male applies himself to the knowledge offered. Most importantly, your understanding of technique and your ear are the most important gifts you can bring to the table. Then throw in a mix of spontaneous creativity and *voilà*...you are on your way to success with these wonderful human beings!

If you can walk you can dance. If you can talk you can sing.

—Zimbabwe Proverb

Make sure the psychological atmosphere is right

Male students will pick up immediately if you are ill at ease. Tell the boy that this is always the most exciting part of your day. He will be more relaxed if you say you love working with the male voice and have great success with it. This immediately gives him a safe place and a feeling of confidence in you as a teacher.

Level the playing field

Don't stand above the male. If anything, have him stand and you sit at the piano. You may also sit at his level if this works for you. Don't be afraid to be goofy and make a fool of yourself. If you have fun, so will he.

Accentuate the positive

Call a boy "guy" or "man" often, even if it appears to be accidental. They will love it. They will rise to whatever standard you set.

Help them to look confident

Many times, audiences look at a certain singer and say to themselves, "He must have a good voice," just because he looks so confident and has great facial expression and posture.

Get to know their names

A great way to start the year is to get to know their names, even if you learn just a few the first days. Everyone likes to know that they're not just a number. When you address them as individuals, the guys will respond much better (and behave much better). Get them involved as individuals, too; ask questions, again asking them to give their name.

Use a familiar song for testing

For the changing voice, use a song like "My Country 'Tis of Thee." For other voices, give them a sheet with the words to "The Star Spangled Banner." This is a difficult song, but revealing as to range and how they handle all aspects of their voice.

Develop your ears and your questions

Every voice is unique and your job is to find that magical button to push that clicks not only with this "man's" voice but also with his personality, which is so closely tied to the voice—he is his instrument. You must look at and listen to the total guy and ask yourself:

- What does this guy's voice lack? Is the voice stifled and stuck inside? Does he need to open his mouth?

- Is the sound thin? He may need to open the space in the back of his mouth and throat.

- Is he nasal? Maybe he needs to try flaring his nostrils a bit: imagine he's smelling the best pizza in the world; think of chipmunk cheeks; fogging goggles; putting air into his sound. Or imagine a hole in the nose/eye area and fill it with sound. All of this opens and energizes the nasal pharynx area.

- Is he singing only in his throat?[6] This, the most common question for inexperienced singers, can be answered by getting the body involved. Have him imagine singing out of his belly button and think of a pushing out feeling.

A voice teacher is no better trained than his ear. His ear is his taste, and his taste is all he can possibly demand of his students.

—Clippinger

---

[6] See "The Four Speakers" on page 107 for other answers for each of these voices.

Keep it simple

Use unison warm-ups at first, incorporating the 5- or 6-note limited range of the changing voices. Buzz on 1-3-5-4-2-7-1. (If the boys find buzzing to be silly, use Muh or Mee.) Go up by half steps, letting the guys switch into head voice if and when they can. Have them put their finger on their Adam's Apple and raise their other hand when it jumps. (Later on, this will be a clue to the larynx jumping, which causes some range and tension issues due to pulling the voice too high with the extrinsic laryngeal muscles.)

Although common at this age in the changing voices, harsh, bright or reedy sounds are unnecessary. Use Oo-oh-ee-ay-ah on 5-4-3-2-1, or begin with Doo or Too. If the group is breathy and weak (also common, but more so in girls), use more Ee-ay-ah-oh-oo (with Mee, also try Dee again). If they sing flat, use an Ee focus; if sharp, switch to an Oo focus.

Improve tone on unison B-flat. Part 3 should sing B-flat just below middle C; Parts 1 and 2 should sing the octave above. Then work on all ten vowel sounds—Dee, Day, Dah, Doh, Doo, Dih, Deh, Da (cat), Duh, Doo (book, look, took). Use "d" before each vowel to get a forward, more speech-like placement at first.

The Four Speakers

The quickest and most powerful visual suggestion that a guy can relate to is to have him imagine himself as a stereo system with four speakers that can help magnify his sound. You need to have many quick, successful fixes to help improve the sound from each "speaker."

Speaker 1—The mouth

- Teeth start together on "n," using B-flat below middle C for changing and changed voices and B-flat the octave above for unchanged voices. He should insert his pointer finger and sing around it on an "ah" vowel so that his teeth are not touching his finger.

- Have him sing "Woa" on a descending 5-note scale. On each note, have him take his right-hand fist and arm and throw it hard out in front of him (as if he is a throwing a shot put). Tell him to let the jaw drop on each note. You may also use "doh." This physical motion helps him to project the tone and forget about producing it in his throat or using old habits.

- Use imagery—visualize the mouth with the elegant spires of a cathedral standing tall inside. Ask if he's ever heard a ventriloquist who sings well.

Speaker 2—The throat

- Most students have the tongue raised and the soft palate lowered, which allows for very little space in the back of the mouth. Tell them to start on the same B-flat "n" as in the mouth exercise above. Instruct them to say "ah," like they do when the doctor asks to see their tonsils. This will pop that space open quickly. Practice will help the muscles to strengthen and keep the throat more open.

- Try tongue push-ups. Start with the "ng" sound (like the end of the word, "sing") and sing, Ng-ah-ng-ah.

- Snort loudly five times. Feel the raise in the soft palate and try to keep it arched while singing an "ah," or any vowel. (Sometimes the more gross the exercise, the more fun the guy has. It also gives you the chance to be goofy, which they will appreciate.)

- Use other familiar visualizations—the beginning of a sneeze or half of a yawn (on both, keep your lips touching), an arch, a dome, an egg, or the feeling of a hot potato while saying, "Wow…that's hot!" Elongate the feeling on the words "wow" and "hot."

- Use "g" or "k" in front of the ten vowels.

Speaker 3—The nasal pharynx (nose/eye area)

- This is the most difficult speaker to feel and understand. Have the guys think "roof focus"—imagining the sound on the roof of his mouth. This also helps intonation when students sing flat, usually occurring on "ah," "oh" and "oo" (hoot) vowels.

- Wrinkle your nose and speak an elongated "ee." Try to make the sound ooze out your nose/eye area and cheeks, like feeling pressure in the front of your face.

- Put your thumb under your upper teeth, drop the jaw, and put fingers 1, 2 and 3 on your forehead, forming a cup or brace. Tip the head slightly and sing into the cup, thinking roof focus and pressure in the front of the face. Remove the brace and sing the vowel with an ugly tone. Then, have the group—all at once when you say "go!"—insert the brace and hear the difference. It's magical! Try on all ten vowels, always going from a bad tone to a beautiful tone. They will want to open those speakers every time to recreate that sound!

- Use "sn," "mee" and "nee," followed by the ten vowels. Make up words. A few examples: sn-i-ckers; sn-ap-ple; Mama mee-ah; pee-za.

Speaker 4—The body

- Sing out of the belly button and think of a pushing out feeling. (A technique borrowed from Pavarotti.)

- Put hands on the side of the ribcage and take a low breath, expanding out against the hands. On every note sung, imagine pressing out or expanding against the hands.

- Use a hiss to quickly build confidence in this, the easiest-to-develop speaker. Have him hiss against a hand both in his lower- and then upper-abdominal muscles; call them the hissing muscles. Have him put his fist against your upper abdomen and you hiss five times, separating each "ss." Move his hand to your lower abdomen and repeat. Then put his fist on his own belly with yours on top of it. Have him hiss five short hisses. Next, have him take a low breath in on an "ah" vowel and expand against the hand, moving it out. Tell him that when he sings abdominal muscle support needs to be activated on every note, whether it's loud or soft. Activating the abdominal muscles will get "body power" under his sound; for guys this is powerful stuff![7]

The changing voice is no big deal, so treat it that way

The voice usually keeps lowering little by little, so you move the boy down to a lower part as this happens. Some may drop quickly, but again, this is just no big deal. Explain to the class that boys at this age are all changing at different times and it would help if the guy would alert you when he is having some difficulty singing the range in his part. Also keep in touch with their ranges with short checks. Have boys come in after class or school every so often. They will appreciate the extra attention and you will get to know the guys even better. More importantly, adjusting the boy's part as he changes keeps him singing successfully.

Make sure to stay positive

The sound of the changing voice is wonderful and unique, having great timbre. Peg Hutson, a middle school teacher at Valley Oak Middle School in Visalia, California, has a plethora of guys in her program and throws a "puberty party" every year. The guys love it. Men who sing come in and speak. They talk about the process of the voice and becoming a man. Then they all eat pizza!

Eventually think of all boys and men as "Baritens" or "Tenibears"

Let them use as much of all parts of their voices as possible, never straining but experimenting. Have them speak in the upper range, elongate the speech, etc. All the pop singers have learned to use their head voice…not falsetto. There are few if any "bass" pop singers. Many of these guys would have been baritones or basses if they only sang in choir. They learn to "cry" and speak in a way that keeps their vocal cords

---

[7] Always be cautious of physical boundaries between teacher and student, particularly when there is a gender difference. Before proceeding with an exercise like this, make sure it's permissible under school policy, and always ask permission before touching a student. If you or they are uncomfortable, put the students in same-gendered pairs and have them work together. Do not force anyone to participate.

together and vibrating. Falsetto doesn't connect to the lower voice, as the vocal cords are not closed and vibrating.

Have them say "Hut 2-3-4" as in a marching cadence. At the close of the hut is a tiny click in the voice. Before taking a breath or letting any air in, they should say "oh" or "ah" or any of the ten vowels in their highest head-voice range. Use the vowels to make up sentences. Ask for their favorite song and speak it in this manner. Have fun making up more sentences. Freedom is the key and the most natural way is to relate singing to speech—singing is elongated speech.

Have the high voices experiment with their lower range by putting their hand on their upper chest and saying a deep, wonderful "mwah" or the French "moi." Have them think of their throats as tiny extensions of their expanded rib cage. Also, think of the throat as a "frog throat" and say "rih-bit" with the opening of the throat. This lowers the larynx a little and allows more ease in accessing some new lower tones. Never force, but do let them experiment.

Adding spin (vibrato)

Important for the long-term care of the voice, spin is also a sign of freedom in the voice. See pages 116–118 for an explanation and specific exercises.

Consider repertoire in a variety of voicings

If you are fortunate to have an all-male choir in middle school, SATB literature is awesome and the best for the voices, as each guy can sing where his *tessitura* best lay. Unfortunately, the parts—and therefore the sections—are labeled "sopranos, altos, tenors, and basses." At this point, it's time to say, "It is as it is. There is so much cool literature in SATB. Get over it." The unison, two-part, TB, and three-part mixed voicings can also work well at this age. Just adapt and look for pieces that fit your group. You can also become an adept arranger, rewriting pieces you and the students like to make them fit the group and its sound.

Know the difference between Three-part Mixed and SAB music

Many music dealers incorrectly combine three-part mixed and SAB music, leading to confusion over the differences. In SAB, the baritone part often goes to low B-flat, or even lower. In three-part mixed, the range of Part 3 is more limited and generally goes no lower than F (or occasionally E) below middle C and no higher than C or D (with the occasional E or E-flat thoughtfully included as cue notes). The use of Part 1, 2 and 3 also enables you to avoid calling your unchanged boys sopranos or altos, which can be a sensitive gender issue with some boys at this age.

Nothing great was ever achieved without enthusiasm.

—Ralph Waldo Emerson

In all situations, pick techniques quickly, move fast, maintain high energy, and above all be enthusiastic!

Working with the Girl's Voice

12

As in the previous chapter, this chapter deals with practical techniques that are usable in the choral setting as well as when working with the individual voice. The choral director is many times the only voice teacher that these students will ever have. The teacher must hone his or her skills in order to be a good mirror for the students to imitate.

Part 1: From a Female Teacher's Perspective

Develop a positive image through good posture

Singers, male and female alike, need to lengthen their instrument, but be aware that girls can be embarrassed by the size of their chest (whether large or small) and will have a tendency to slouch. Remind girls that posture affects the voice and breathing, and therefore tone. Focus on what her body language is saying to others and what it's saying to her own self-image. How a singer stands is how she will think and sing.

Exercises to improve posture include:

- Slump. Put the hand on the upper chest and gradually lift the upper body. This gives room to the lungs and space to the rib cage for breathing.

- Raise right arm and hand toward the ceiling while standing on your tiptoes. Move back and forth on your toes, stretching the side and ribcage with each step. Repeat with left arm. When done, move shoulders back gently and rest relaxed. You'll feel like you've grown an inch!

- Lift arms until they are parallel to the floor, with palms facing down. Bend at the elbow, bring palms towards the body. Pull elbows and arms back gently three times. On the fourth time, let the arms fall open and away from you. Repeat the sequence three times.

Mix it up; have a choir of "Sopraltos" and "Altanos" rather than sopranos and altos

Sopranos never learn to sing harmony and don't develop as keen of an ear. And while altos become great readers, they don't learn to use and develop their full voice. Avoiding traditional labels alleviates any psychological hang-ups some girls and women may develop dealing with their range.

Also, there are very few true altos, even in high school. Most have never learned to use, much less strengthen, their upper voice. They have pulled the extrinsic laryngeal muscles and developed a large break when going from chest voice to head voice. Don't reinforce the psychological hurdles to overcoming this break by addressing chest, middle and head voices; instead think of the voice as one big mix.

The Ten Vowels

The ten vowels, with a "d" in front of each to bring it present in the mouth as in speech, are as follows: D<u>ee</u>, D<u>ay</u>, D<u>ah</u>, D<u>oh</u>, D<u>oo</u> (hoot), D<u>ih</u>, D<u>eh</u>, D<u>a</u> (cat), D<u>uh</u>, and D<u>oo</u> (book, look, took). While the first five are common, the latter vowels are more unusual and are frequent trouble spots.

The ten vowels can be used in a variety of exercises:

- To learn the vowels, have students (male and female) go through their music and write the primary vowel sounds over each word or syllable. This can be done individually or as a class activity and will become easier with practice.

- Sing a C-major scale on "dee," beginning on middle C, ascending and descending. The "ee" vowel keeps the tone forward and the "d" brings it present in the mouth as in speech. To keep her from starting in her head voice, have her imagine that she has a pouch under her chin like a pelican. Instead of holding fish, her pouch holds her tone. This helps to keep the larynx from rising, which, in turn, helps develop a smooth, connected voice. Continue to do this exercise, moving up by half steps until reaching E-flat or F. This exercise is also effective in the higher ranges as well, although some vowel sounds may need to be modified slightly.

- Other imagery to improve the ten vowels: imagine the neck as a tiny extension of your expanded rib cage and think of the throat as a frog's throat, saying "rih-bit" then "ree-bit" then "ray-bit," until you have practiced "frog throat" on all ten vowels. Think of breathing out through the vowel in the mouth

Ride the breath and use the body for support

Female students tend not to be as physical in their approach to singing. They sing either in their throat in chest voice, pulling the wrong extrinsic laryngeal muscles up and developing a bad break, or in head voice, disconnected from their lower range and lacking the colors that add so much to the richness of their sound. Placement of the tone and the improper opening of The Four Speakers[8] contribute to this problem, but a more significant factor is lack of support. The more work the abdominal muscles do, the less work the throat needs to do.

- *Filling the lungs.* Have the singer close one nostril with her finger. Take a deep breath. Once up to capacity, sing and count as far as possible on one pitch.

- *Expand the ribcage and belly.* With your hands open in the shape of an "L," place them on your abdomen, slightly above the waistline. The fingers should just touch in front; the thumbs should point toward the back. Blow all your air out. Open the throat in the shape of an "ah," inhale

[8] See pages 107–110 for a description of "The Four Speakers" and exercises to help open them while singing.

and expand the fingers and thumbs with the low breath. Sing and count as you exhale.

- *Expand through the back.* With the hands around the waist, thumbs in front, fingers around the back, bend over as if touching your toes. Open mouth and throat in the shape of an "ah," breathe in, expanding through the back. Stand up, sing and count. Repeat the exercise, but only bend until your torso is parallel with the floor. Repeat, this time bending only 45 degrees. Then, try to get the same feeling standing up and breathing low and through the back. Sing and count each time.

- *Sit and breathe.* Put your chin in your hands and your elbows on your knees. Open throat in the shape of an "ah" and breathe. Feel the expansion through the back and into the lower body. Sing and count. This is a great way to establish proper breathing in a seated rehearsal.

Know how and when to add spin (vibrato)

Keeping the vocal cords taut doesn't produce a healthy voice. They must be loose and freely moving, like waves in the water. The resulting spin, unpopular amongst many choral directors, who feel it detracts from a good choral blend, is nonetheless important for the long-term care of the voice. It also creates the energized sound that most untrained voices lack. Exercises to add spin and free the voice include:

- *Slinky spin.* Have the student use the pointer finger to create big wide, crazy loops from the forehead to the bottom of the nose. Sing a sustained "ee" on a higher pitch—B-flat below middle C for changed voices; third-line B-flat for treble voices. Spin wildly like the big loops of a slinky going down the stairs. Stay close to the face.

- *Panting.* This exercise teaches students that the tone and spin come from the support system, not the throat. Eventually, the neuromuscular system takes over and the vibrato begins to happen automatically. First, we must get the voice to loosen, thus the body movement. Second, we must train the ear to hear the spin of the tone.

1. Pant with no sound twice, then three times, then four times, then five times, increasing to thirteen times.

2. Pant with a slightly phonated sound twice, then three times, etc. as above.

3. Pulse twice on a vowel, such as "ee," using a speech tone. Repeat, pulsing three times, then four times, then five times, increasing to thirteen times. Do not put an "h" between vowels. The sound should be one tone with tiny pulses from the hissing muscles. You may speed it up or slow it down. Repeat for all ten vowels.

4. Pulse again on a vowel, but on actual pitches throughout the range, i.e. 1-5-8 of a scale.

- *Push forward.* Set your arms as if getting ready to push something away—arms bent at the elbow, in front of the body, palms facing forward. Move arms forward in a jerky, pushing motion away from the body while sustaining a vowel or pitch on "duh," or a vowel of choice.

- *Play the violin.* Put the four fingers of your right hand on the top of your left hand. Move them back and forth like you are producing a vibrato on a string instrument.

- *The Heart Monitor.* This exercise is ideal to learn to control vibrato so that it can be added or removed at will. Touch the pointer finger of the right hand to the front of the left shoulder. As you sing a pitch (the same B-flat mentioned earlier), make a wide zigzag with your finger as you pull it across your body. Be wild and very physical; this physical action loosens the voice. Now move the finger in a straight line from the right of your body to the left, letting the tone of the voice straighten to match the straight line made by the finger.

Breathiness can be cured!

One of the most common complaints among choral directors is that girls are so breathy. Begin to solve the problem with these exercises:

- *Swallow.* Then, before you can let air enter the throat, say, "I like you!" Once the initial phonation on the "I" is started, you can open the throat because the chords are now properly closed and vibrating without air escaping between them.

- *Say the marching cadence, "Hut 2-3-4."* At the close of the "hut" is a tiny click in the voice. Before taking a breath or letting any air in, say "oh" or "ah" or any of the ten vowels in your highest head voice.

- *Hissing and* staccato *"dees."* Hiss three times and then sing three *staccato* "dees" on one pitch, preferably B-flat. Hold the third "dee" and sing, also on "dee," 5-4-3-2-1. End on "dah."

- *Use witchy sounds.* Speak the ten vowels in a higher range with the nose wrinkled, trying to get as witchy, bright and nasty as possible. Use the hissing muscles as the initial attack with each.

- *Use more abdominal support.* This will help to close the vocal cords and not allow air to escape.

Part 2: From a Male Teacher's Perspective

A male teacher working with the female's voice can be one of the biggest challenges when teaching chorus. What may work for one male teacher may not work for another. Many times we hear how a female teacher has trouble working with the boy's voice. The same challenges can take place for the male teacher working with the girl's voice. Here are a few pointers to help overcome some of these challenges.

Girls often try to "out sing" one another

This can be a problem not only within the girls' sections, but also between the boys' and the girls' sections. The male director can tell the girls, from his point of view, how important it is for everyone to conform their individual voices for the benefit of the entire ensemble. The director must always remind the students that singing in a chorus is different from singing alone.

Use the word "blend" and remind the girls to do this often when singing in a chorus

The word "blend" seems to work best when trying to produce a well-balanced carpet of sound in the choral ensemble. Just think of a blender—you put diverse ingredients, be they solid or liquid, in a blender and it produces a consistent thickness and texture.

"I sang soprano."

You may have a newly placed alto or two explain to you that they "sang soprano" in their previous choir or with the previous teacher. What this singer may be suggesting is that she would *rather* sing soprano, or that she liked her previous teacher better, or that she would rather sit by her friends, in the soprano section. This problem can be nipped in the bud by saying, "Oh, that's great, because now you'll learn to sing a whole new part in a whole new section!" Avoid the reply, "Well, I say you are an alto." This plays into her hand and creates the beginnings of a conflict. Under no circumstances, though, should you allow the singer to get her way. Not only does it set a dangerous precedent, it tells the class that you do not have confidence in what you're doing and are willing to let the students take charge and control the class. Stick to your decision and remember that changes can always be made here and there quickly and quietly as the year goes on, when the time is right.

Have other female students model the tone, especially those girls who are singing the tone you desire

The male teacher modeling a sound for a female student may not get the desired result so choose a girl or two to model for the rest of the singers. After the girls (and the entire group) sing, the male director can adjust accordingly. Using a female student to model a tone can also work well when getting boys to sing on pitch because they will hear a different tone quality. One reason for this phenomenon is because it's an octave higher and, as the boys hear, they may produce their sound with more ease.

Sing with the tone you desire to hear from the girls, but sing it in your range (and therefore an octave lower than the girls' part)

When the male teacher sings in his comfortable range, the girls see the physical way the male teacher is singing. They will also hear his tone quality and will model their voices after his example. When the male teacher sings in falsetto, girls will often see and hear the sound differently and try to mimic this falsetto on the same pitch but in their octave, resulting in an undesirable tone. If you can sing in the falsetto without any physical strain on face, body and vocal apparatus, it may be a suitable model. With either approach, be sure to model in a tone that discourages the girls from producing a harsh, strident sound. This sound may be fine for the solo voice, but it's a detriment to a beautiful, well-balanced choral tone.

Developing Musicianship in the Choral Classroom

13

Ear training: The key to the door of musicianship

Just as the body needs to be exercised for overall physical development, the ears—which are connected to the mind's entire learning process—need to be exercised for overall mental and musical development. While training as a choral educator, ear training—a.k.a. aural skills, a.k.a. sight singing, a.k.a. [insert your college or university's name for it]—was a core music class. Its significant place in your degree program should speak to its importance, for the better trained your ear is, the better your musicianship will be. The same is true for your students. The better their listening skills, the better their choral instincts, preventing possible problems and allowing more time and energy to work on more difficult aspects of the choral music.

Exercise 1: Teach the students to identify intervals.

Students quickly and easily learn intervals while they are singing vocal exercises, choral warm-ups or the choral music itself. After that, it's a matter of identifying the intervals, making the connection with what they are hearing, naming the interval, and applying this skill to reading the music. Of course, there are mnemonic devices to be found in familiar tunes—the theme from *Jaws* is a minor second; "My Bonnie Lies Over the Ocean" includes a major sixth. If these devices are effective when teaching intervals, use them!

A true exercise, which can be effectively taught in even ten minutes, is as follows:

- Teach 3 or 4 intervals. A good place to start is teaching the perfect octave, the major third, the perfect fifth, and the perfect fourth. Play these intervals several times until the students get them in their ears. Make any connections you can to previously learned material.

- Play an interval and call on a student to identify it. Continue this process. Every student in the class will be quiet because they are mentally and aurally preparing in case they are called upon.[9]

- Make a game out of identifying the intervals. You can divide the class between boys and girls or between sections. Keep track of which section's students identified the most intervals correctly. You will be surprised at how fun and exciting ear training is for everyone!

- Have a friendly competition between a student, designated by the class, and the teacher. Have the class guess who will win before the activity begins. It is a good way to build camaraderie!

When finding ten minutes for this exercise, consider that aural exercises at the beginning of the rehearsal are a terrific way to help students focus. You can take ten minutes from the middle of the rehearsal to break up any monotony. Or you can use this exercise to close the rehearsal with something useful and meaningful.

If you have certain vocal exercises, or can find a part of a choral piece that you are working with, this will be even better because you are making a connection with what the students have learned while developing their mental and aural skills. Also, it validates what you are teaching. Students love to have examples of why what you are teaching is important, and if you make any connection between something you've

---

[9] Do *not* reverse this process by first calling on a student and then playing the interval. If you do, all of the students who weren't called will consider themselves "off the hook" and will shut their minds and their ears for this interval. Keep this same phenomenon in mind whenever you teach—present the question to the entire class, then call on the individual.

previously taught and something you're teaching now, it's powerful and helps you further grasp and get command of your students' intellect.

Exercise 2: Sing intervals back from the piano

Try one of these two activities: 1) Have one student sing an interval and call on another student to identity it or 2) Play one note and ask a student or the class to sing a certain interval above it.

Exercise 3: Identify the major and minor (natural, harmonic and melodic) scales

Find five or ten minutes of your choral rehearsal to play the four scales—major, natural minor, harmonic minor, and melodic minor. Once the students are familiar with these scales, simply play one and call on a student to identify it. After some time, you can use a simple test to quiz the students on what they have learned.

Choral listening exercises

Another fun and exciting way to help train your students' ears is to introduce and acquaint them to many different choral performance groups, whether it's at a live performance or from an audio or video recording. However, be aware that one sure way to bore or even turn off your students to choral music is to play an example without first guiding their listening. Use any of the following examples to engage your students and focus their concentration, and hopefully spark their interest in choral music for a lifetime.

Exercise 1: Discerning between monophonic, homophonic, polyphonic, and unison singing.

First, you need to teach your students what each is and how it differs from the others:

- *Monophonic*—one sound. In choral terms, one person singing. It can also mean everyone singing the exact same melody together, on the exact same notes. Play an example of one person singing and an example of more than one person singing monophonically.

- *Homophonic*—same sound; more than one person singing the same words in the same rhythm but in harmony. This can be referred to as *chordal style* or *hymn style*. Homophonic also refers to one or more persons singing with an accompaniment. That accompaniment can be instrumental or it can be another section in the choir providing an accompaniment while another section sings the melody.

- *Polyphonic*—many sounds; two or more voices singing independent parts at the same time. It's like a round, but more complicated. Play an example of polyphonic music. You may want to begin with polyphony between distinctive voices, such as men and women each singing a part.

- *Unison*—one interval; a group of persons singing the same part (monophonic unison) or men and women singing the same part an octave apart. Play an example of the latter. Do not bother with the monophonic unison; it will not necessarily help the learning process at this particular time.

Once you explain the differences to your students and have played examples, you can use these terms when introducing choral music that they are singing or listening to. Have a fun aural quiz—play an example and have students identify it as monophonic, homophonic, polyphonic, or unison. The goal is not to trick your students, rather it is to help them better understand what they are listening to.[10] Once they achieve a better understanding of choral music, they will appreciate it that much more and sing that much better in your chorus!

Exercise 2: Adjudication

When you are listening to recorded choral examples, stop every now and then to discuss what you are listening to. Are the voices blending well? Are there any dynamic contrasts?

---

[10] These terms and concepts can become very complicated if you want them to be. This is not the time to show how smart you are as a choral director, but rather a time to show how wise, prudent and considerate you are as an educator.

How old do you think the choir members are? Overall, what do you like or dislike about what you are listening to?

Exercise 3: Exchange concerts or performances

Invite other choirs to sing at your school or travel to other schools to sing for each other. Be open about the performances. Discuss with each other what you liked and what, if any, areas could use some improvement.

Exercise 4: Introduce and teach the instruments of the band and orchestra

When you teach your students about the instruments in the band and orchestra, they will gain a better understanding of the instruments in the choir. There will always be a time when your students will see and hear a choral performance that includes an orchestra, like an oratorio or a symphony. Further, there will most likely be a time when your students will sing with a band or orchestra. The foundation laid in your class will help them better understand these ensembles.

Exercise 5: Identifying styles in choral music

Teach your students the identifiable stylistic differences between music of different periods, like Baroque, Classical and Romantic, and different genres or types, like madrigals, spirituals and patriotic selections. This knowledge will give students something to latch on to, helping them listen more intently and objectively. Be sure to begin with examples that are very easy to discern, giving students the important feeling of success and building their interest in choral music.

Sight reading: The key to lifelong learning in music

Just as teaching students to read opens their paths to lifelong learning, teaching students to read music opens their paths to lifelong musical learning. Sight reading doesn't have to be the time when the students get out a book of sight-singing examples. Rather, there are fun and exciting ways to get your students reading music, and learning how to sight read.

Exercise 1: Solfège hand signals

These signals are great because the students can do them along with the teacher. It can also help the students keep their minds occupied, making sight reading and ear training more fun and exciting.

Exercise 2: Rhythm-reading exercises

You can put a few measures on the board or overhead and the students can clap the rhythms. You can even have a "rhythm of the day" as a sponge activity. Students will learn to love reading and clapping rhythms.

Exercise 3: Taking dictation

Students can be trained to write down what they hear, and the sooner they do, the better. Even if the students do not write down exactly what they hear, mold and shape the students as they move in the right direction. This can include notating big picture elements correctly, like the general shape of the melody, whether it ascends or descends, for example, and the differences between quicker notes, like eighths and quarters, and slower notes, like halves and wholes.

Exercise 4: Using manipulatives

Create cards with a variety of note and rest values and bar lines. Play a rhythm and ask a student to use these cards to notate the rhythm on the board. This is a fun way for the students to learn, and everyone will want to have a chance to go to the board and put up a rhythm.

In addition to the above examples, there are many books with lessons, games and methods to teach sight reading. You can use as many of these as you would like. While it's usually best to use the methods you are most comfortable teaching, don't limit yourself or your students; learn in as many different ways as possible.

Kinesthetics: Give those energized kids a chance to move!

Although most teachers are aware of teaching to the different learning styles of students, the students who are most often forgotten are those who just can't sit still. Well, using movement in your rehearsals and lessons is just for them! It's also just plain good for the mind and body, and for helping the two work together.

One very popular method of teaching music through movement is the Dalcroze method, Eurythmics. Eurythmics, which means "good rhythm," is a systematic process of teaching the body to combat rhythmic problems found in the actual music. A method so broad there are degree programs specializing in it, the following is not intended to be a comprehensive presentation of Dalcroze Eurythmics. Rather, it provides a few concrete examples that you can use in your choral rehearsal. From here, it's up to you to determine the rhythmic problems in the music and expand this method to best solve them.

Exercise 1: Counterpoint as a way of phrasing

While singing "My Country 'Tis of Thee," step the rhythm of the melody on the risers, alternating feet. Clap on the off-beat melody note. Once the pattern is comfortable, flip the movement between the hands and the feet.

An exercise like this can really help the flow and line of a melody. Often, singers want to sing phrases in a choppy way. Instilling counterpoint in a physical way using movement will address this problem.

Exercise 2: Pulling each others' sections while singing a choral piece

Take the example of John Rutter's "All Things Bright and Beautiful":

Hill and Vale...
Hill and Vale
And Tree and Flower...
And Tree and Flower

Put the sopranos, altos, tenors, and basses in a line. Each section will step forward while they are singing their respective part. When they are holding their last note, the section looks back and physically pulls the next singer forward as if he or she is on a rope. This simple example and movement help physically illustrate polyphonic music—each part is independent, yet they work together to keep the entire choral piece functioning as one.

This can be easily applied in rehearsals by using the hands and face instead of the feet. When one section is finishing its phrase, instruct that section to literally pass—with eye contact and a toss of the hands—its phrase to the section that is taking over the phrase. This is a great way for the choral singers to get into the habit of listening to each other instead of just their own part.

Exercise 3: Everyone on the same rhythmic page

Sometimes when the chorus is singing, it can seem as though one section of the chorus is not feeling the same beat or rhythm as the other. There are several movement exercises that can be done to solve this problem:

- Everyone puts their hand on the shoulder of the person to their right. As the chorus is singing, each student is tapping the rhythm of the music on their neighbor's shoulder. Theoretically, a chain is formed and everyone feels the same rhythm.
- Each student exchanges the hands from the top to the bottom (something like exchanging a ball from the right hand to the left in a vertical motion). The conductor leads the class as the chorus is singing.
- The conductor or students in the chorus can bounce a tennis ball in rhythm. The teacher can also show the time-space relationship with different tempos.

Computer technology

There is software to help your students read music and develop their listening and memory skills. If your school has a computer lab, or even one available computer, take advantage of everything that is out there in today's world!

Rehearsing for Musical Success

14

Don't over-rehearse a brand new piece of music

When beginning a new piece of music, work on it for a short time and put it away. You may want to go over a section or two to help familiarize your students with the music, but resist pushing it to the point where the students become disinterested, which is a perfectly natural reaction to the unfamiliar. Even with limited exposure, the students will have the music in the back of their minds and it will incubate from there. The next time you take out the piece, it will no longer be a new, unfamiliar piece and the students will experience more success, helping them to better enjoy the piece. Further, when you take out this, the now second-newest piece of music, they will really take ownership of it because it's "one that they already know."

The same goes for working on a difficult passage. Don't harp on something that's going wrong. Instead, give it a rest. When you come back to it a day or so later, you will be pleasantly surprised to find that this passage which was never done correctly before somehow magically worked the first time it was attempted. There may be many reasons for this, but one is that with a new day often comes a fresh mind that is more capable of tackling a problem than it was before.

Teach the text in the rhythm of the music

If you are teaching the text of a foreign language, say the text in the rhythm of the music and the students will catch on much faster. If you simply talk through the rhythms to be repeated back by the students, they will often just mumble the words back. However, if you say the text in rhythm with a spunky enthusiasm, you will catch everyone's attention and break up any monotony in your rehearsal.

You can use this same technique if you are going over any tricky rhythm, even if the text is in English. You can also instruct your students to beat the rhythm (or the steady tempo) with their hand against their leg or by tapping their foot. You can take this a step further by having your students beat the steady tempo with their feet while speaking and tapping the rhythm.

Keep a rhythm going in your rehearsal with your voice and your body language

When you are in rehearsal, you can raise the enthusiasm level a few notches by keeping the rhythm going in your speech or piano playing. Here are specific examples:

- When you have completed rehearsing a section of the chorus, keep your conducting pattern going without missing a beat. In the tempo of the music (and your conducting), say, "Great job... altos!...Basses...same section... ready...breathe...here we...go!" This was all spoken in eight beats and by the ninth beat, the basses are singing on the downbeat. This can really snuff out any apathy that may otherwise enter your room.

- Follow the same idea as above when you are playing the piano, but instead of keeping a steady conducting pattern, keep a steady beat in the piano. You don't necessarily have to speak in rhythm if you are playing a steady pattern on the piano but you still give directions enthusiastically, within a small time frame and within the context of the rhythm.

The two examples above sure beat the old "Okay, altos, sit down. Now I would like the basses to stand up and sing the same section, which is at the top of page 3, starting on the 2nd measure, on the first beat...No, basses, that's way too noisy...how are you going to sing well if you don't breathe properly," etc., etc.

Use simple yet effective breathing exercises

1. Blowing air into a closed fist

A simple, yet effective breathing exercise is to blow air into your fist (like a quarterback does on a cold day). The purpose of the technique is to help connect the breath to the sound production mechanism, helping to alleviate a breathy tone. It can also help build the diaphragm for better breath control. This technique is simple enough for anybody to do, helps get the choral students immediately focused and working together, and is an easy way to get the choral rehearsal started quickly and efficiently.

2. Bending over to breathe

One way to get the students to inhale in the proper place is to have them gently bend over and breathe in. The inhaled air will automatically go where it's suppose to go. Once the students have experienced this sensation, have them stand up slightly more and repeat the inhalation. Repeat until the students are standing up tall and feel where they are breathing. They can go at their pace, and will learn much faster because they are teaching themselves through their own experimentation.

3. Begin your breathing with exhalation

Play an organized game to get your students to exhale all of their air. Direct the students to:

- Exhale on 4 counts of "Sh-sh-sh-sh"

- Hiss for 8 counts

- "Blow out candles," with the pointer finger as the candle, for 4 or 8 counts

- Hiss for 8 counts

- Exhale on 4 counts of "K-k-k-k," etc., until they are completely out of breath.

At this point, instruct the students to gently breathe in. The air goes exactly where it's suppose to go because the body automatically uses the air as efficiently as possible and knows to place it where it's most needed and most useful. This is the same place where the air belongs for a proper breath for the best tone production.

4. Hands on while expanding the rib cage

Instruct the students to place their hands above their hips near the bottom of the rib cage. The fingers can be pointed to the front, towards the belly button, or reversed, with thumbs out and fingers on the back of the rib cage. Explain that the ribs are bones that can actually expand and contract, which makes them different from any other bones in their body. Students will find this interesting and it will further spark their interest in the exercise (and diffuse any thoughts of "this is stupid").

Ask the students to take a nice big breath while expanding the rib cage. They should feel their hands move away from the body. When they have inhaled and the ribs are fully expanded, instruct the students to hiss out their air while keeping the ribs fully expanded. Practice this a few times until the students get the hang of it.

5. Always breathe in as a slight yawn or a "surprised" sensation

The first time you hear any noise as your choir takes a deep breath should be the last time you hear that audible breath noise. Simply explain to your singers that if you breathe in making that noise, it will sound horrible, dry out the throat and close up the sound. You must never hear it again! (This type of verbalizing the negative is totally non-threatening, so in this case, it's okay to use.) Instead, instruct the students to breathe in like a slight yawn and a feeling of being surprised (with the big eyes and everything).

To help your students visualize and feel this sensation of raising the soft palate, you can tell them this story:

> How many times have you gone out to eat pizza with your family or friends? The minute the pizza is placed on the table, you face a dilemma. You can wait patiently for the pizza to cool before eating, or you can dive in and eat now. If you wait, others around you may get more! Further, you are starving and want to eat now! If you choose to dive in and eat that piping hot pizza, you must eat it with an open mouth and with the back of our throat open to help cool the pizza.

Ask the students to remember this sensation while they are singing. They will sing with a relaxed open throat. Others may ask the students to imagine they have a hot potato in their mouth. Some may use the marble in the back of the throat technique. Do whatever works for you because there's no right or wrong way when you are making an analogy. An analogy doesn't have to be physically possible or make a lot of sense. If it gets the required results—go for it!

6. Always breathe in as if you are singing an "Ah" vowel

When the choral singers are inhaling to sing, the back of their throat should always remain like an open "Ah," even when they are singing other vowels. This will keep the throat relaxed and consistent while producing a full, yet beautiful tone. The formation of the other vowel sounds, as well as the consonants, has to do with the front of the mouth and not the back of the throat.

7. Breathe "hot air" on the hand while singing

As the choral students are singing, have them place a hand in front of their mouth as if breathing hot air on a cold mirror. Tell them the hotter the air, the better the tone. Practice this a few times. While they are singing like this, they will hear a much more uniform sound with a lovely tone. After doing this several times, have the students put their hands by their sides, but ask them to remember the sensation they had when their hand was up. When you hear a tone that needs refining, simply ask the choir students to sing with more hot air on the hand. They will automatically produce a more beautiful tone without raising their hand.

Use vertical conducting gestures for a tall sound

Many potential problems can be alleviated simply by using more vertical conducting gestures. It will get your students to stand up taller and prevent vowels from spreading. It will also keep the focal point compact and closer to the body, where the breath is generated. Also, have your students conduct along with you while they are singing. This will help them to kinesthetically connect their body with their internal sound. When the students are involved physically with their singing, it really helps loosen up their vocal mechanism and prevents any lethargy. For concerts and rehearsals, the students will make a better connection with you as the conductor and they will internalize your conducting gestures, producing a better individual, and in turn, choral tone.

Use circular conducting gestures for proper breath support

When you use a circular motion with your hands and arms in front of the waist, you are demonstrating a way for your chorus to take a deep, functional breath that they can use for a better sound. The students can practice this with you often. As they are "conducting" in a circular motion, have them breathe in for 4 beats before singing. In performance, they will breathe much better and stand taller, producing a beautiful sound.

Use a bounce for a cutoff to allow the music to keep singing

When you have a bounce point for a cutoff and continue to raise your hands in an "up in smoke" motion, you will alleviate a cutoff that abruptly stops the sound of the music. If you bounce the cutoff and continue with a gesture that lets the sound continue to flow with an echoing reverberation effect, the choir will have a more victorious release and everyone will hear the flowing beauty of the music. Have your students practice this release with everyone participating in the conducting. The resulting internalization will allow the chorus to be more successful in performance with a better internalization of the music.

Use a rainbow arch to make a phrase beautiful

The arched phrase—one which starts gently, grows through the phrase and ends gently—is a frequent goal of directors. Even though directors may ask for an arched phrase (and even gesture it with their hands) the result will be better accomplished if the students gesture a rainbow arch themselves while singing. When the students make a rainbow arch, make sure the gesture is nice and big, and made with sincerity. As the students practice this gesture, they will internalize it and will now sing beautiful phrases the next time the director uses this same gesture in his conducting.

Nothing is particularly hard if you divide it into small jobs.

—Henry Ford

When you are teaching SATB music, straight up or with *divisi*, it can seem like a massive task, especially for the middle school chorus teacher. However, approaching it as breaking the music into small sections and putting it together piece by piece, can make teaching, as well as learning, challenging SATB music a reality. If, as the director, you are fully prepared and know the music inside and out, you can teach it to the individual sections rather easily. Once the individual sections are learning their parts, by themselves and within the context of singing together with one or more sections, it's up to you to put it all together.

Cast the tone to a focal point

Most choral students will sing with only the energy necessary to allow them to hear themselves singing. Some will give enough to sing as far as the director, but all students need to learn how to sing as far as the audience or to the back of the auditorium. There are several visuals and kinesthetic ideas you can use to teach this concept:

- *Cast a fishing line into a lake as far as possible and sing that area*—This will help the students open the vocal mechanism and sing with more energy.

- *Throw a Frisbee®*—This will help the students sing with more flow in their phrases.

- *Throw a football and point with the follow through*—This will help the students better match a pitch.

- *Throw a baseball at a focal point in the room*—This will help students wind up energy and sing with more spirit.

Make your vocal exercises parallel the music you are rehearsing

If a physical therapist helping to rehabilitate a patient after knee surgery does stretching and weight training for the arms, is he helping the patient walk again? Find those areas that are causing vocal troubles or difficulties in the choral music and then use exercises that pertain to these areas in the music, or develop your own vocal exercises that are consequential to what you are doing.

A related note about vocal exercises or warm-ups—doing the same exercise day in and day out can quickly become pointless.

Get your students physically involved in warm-ups

When chorus students move, they think less and sing more naturally. Like anything, if you introduce this in a practical way, without making a big thing out of it, all students will move freely on the risers or around the room. It can really energize a rehearsal.

Whenever possible, make any learning fun

Everything from teaching rudiments of music to teaching parts to a section can seem monotonous to any student, so make the learning fun whenever possible. This doesn't mean that everything you teach is or should be *all* fun and games. Rather, it means to break up monotony where possible. In fact, if everything becomes all fun and games, then "fun and games" itself can become monotonous!

Sometimes you have to change a note

If the music on the paper doesn't fit a section's voice range, go ahead and write your own notes within the context of the chord. Too many choral teachers get hung up on singing exactly what is on the paper. When you are working with young voices, however, this is simply not always possible. This shouldn't hinder you from singing advanced literature. Remember that we are here to help advance the students' education. They will be able to sing those notes later, when they mature and their voices develop further.

The trampoline effect

Ask students to sing while moving their hands and arms as if jumping on a trampoline. This trampoline effect helps students visualize their singing while producing a long phrase and energizes one note to the next. It also helps loosen their vocal apparatus and helps them to produce an open, free tone. The conductor can then use her gestures while the students are singing and the students will follow well and produce beautiful, sensitive, yet energized phrases.

Traveling hands to flow from one phrase to another

First of all, traveling hands is the signal a basketball coach makes when the player is whistled for traveling. You can call this gesture whatever you want. Similar to the trampoline effect, it helps a phrase keep its flow. Also, you can use this if one section is singing and the musical emphasis goes to another section. The first section can use this gesture and hand their phrase to another section, who will hand it to the next, etc.

March in place three times

Choir students have probably heard "stand up straight" so many times that they have long since tuned out these three words. Also, many students (especially girls) like to stand with one hip off to the side. Instead of fighting these tendencies, say, "march in place three times." Just watch and see how quickly and cooperatively the students stand up tall!

Selecting Your Choral Repertoire

Selecting the "right" music for your choirs is one of the most difficult aspects of any director's job. You must take into account many factors, including your teaching philosophies and long-term vision of the program, programming balance, educational benefits to your students, enjoyment of your audience, and accessibility to your singers. *And* you likely have to make all of these decisions at least a year in advance because of district budget deadlines.

Ability of the singers

Before you even begin to consider music selection, you must have a realistic understanding of the ability of your singers. You must also target any trouble spots in your choir and select music that addresses and helps improve them.

A common problem in many developing two-part choirs is that many students will sing the "other" part, or worse yet, will have no concept of harmonization. A great way to alleviate this problem before it has a chance to begin is to select two-part music where each part sings independently for a portion of the arrangement. Typically, this is achieved with echoing or back and forth singing, and it really helps the students get the concept of two separate parts. These arrangements will usually include a phrase or verse where there is absolute homophonic singing, usually in thirds. By the time you arrive at this section, the students are more secure and hopefully better prepared to execute this singing.

If you have a mixed choir with developing boys' voices, make sure that you are choosing SAT or three-part mixed literature instead of SAB literature.

If you want to sing more challenging SATB music, one of your biggest responsibilities is making sure that the music is learnable and singable by the entire ensemble, and that it's accessible to the range of the basses. This is such an important requirement when selecting music that you may want to make a first pass, eliminating any titles that are not accessible to your group, and then make the rest of your evaluations and decisions on only those that remain.

Challenges

While you should never risk the disasters and feelings of failure that come with choosing music that has no chance of being performed successfully, students should be presented with challenges. This is particularly true for middle school students, who are at a time in their lives when they should explore their abilities and discover what they are made of.

Do not feel ashamed if you make an attempt at challenging literature and perform it to the best of the ability of you and your students. Perhaps the students will reexamine the music later on, say in high school, and then they will realize how they were challenged in middle school. This will instill pride in the students and your program and will encourage them to pursue further challenges in other areas of their lives. The foundation laid in middle school will also help them better perform the piece—and other pieces like it—in high school. (Of course, so will their physical, mental and musical maturation; none of which you could control when these students were in middle school.)

You will certainly gain your students' respect and loyalty for respecting them enough to present a challenge. Just be careful not to overreach or make every piece a challenge. Use an ultimately challenging piece as a stepping stone for future success. They may or may not grasp all elements of the work, but always allow the latitude for the students to surprise you. You never know, what may seem extremely challenging on paper may not be extremely challenging to sing. And never underestimate middle school students—they are full of surprises, including the ability to perform well beyond your wildest imagination!

Success can also hinge entirely on presentation. When you are introducing a challenging piece of music, don't make it seem as such. Saying to the students, "this piece is rather difficult but I thought we'd try it anyway," may be the only thing that hinders a realistic and practical attempt at successfully learning the music and performing it at its optimal level.

What are they learning?

As choral educators, we must always consider the educational benefit, or lack thereof, of a given piece. The music's text is an often-overlooked source of these teaching opportunities. Is it a famous poem? Does it explore an interesting subject? Is it in a foreign language? Many elements can open a window to discussion or even interdisciplinary teaching, which allows you to get other teachers and departments involved in your choral program. Also consider specific performance needs as they relate to text subject—graduation, farewells, patriotic occasions, dedications, etc.

An important footnote to any discussion of text is addressing texts with a religious connotation. While religious elements should not hinder your selection, it's important that you present it in a prudent, non-sectarian way. Instead of dwelling on the text itself, allow the meaning of the text to happen naturally by the way you phrase the music and develop its overall structure. Take care to avoid emphasizing the text for the text's sake. You may want to select text in Latin, not only because it defrays any potential problem, but also because you can work on the pure vowel sounds in Latin. They can easily be transferred to texts in the English language to make them sound more beautiful and appropriate to the music, regardless of musical style.

Once you have considered the text in selecting your pieces, you can now move to the music itself. You will want to look at the overall structure of the piece, including melodic lines and the harmonization of the sections (sopranos/altos, tenors/basses; sopranos/basses, alto/tenors, etc.).

Ask yourself the following questions:

- Does the structure of the piece lead to sections helping other sections, if necessary for the development of your choirs?
- Are individual sections able to sing by themselves?
- Are your students ready for polyphonic music?
- Do you want to introduce *a cappella* music? If so, does this piece have a piano accompaniment with an *a cappella* middle section?

Speaking of accompaniment, do you have an accompanist who is able to play the music you've chosen? How many times have you heard a choir sing and it's apparent that the accompanist is struggling, actually detracting from the musicality of the chorus? It's not fair to you or your choir if the accompanist is not playing to the ability of the ensemble nor even playing the written notes in a musical, expressive way. However, it's the responsibility of the director to find an accompanist who has the ability to play the chosen music, or to choose music that you know the available accompanist is able to play well.

Balanced program

You will likely find good, educationally sound repertoire that fulfills your needs in every conceivable style, including Broadway, show or pop, classical, original concert repertoire, spirituals, and folk arrangements, be they American or multicultural. While you should be cautious of selecting music just for the sake of filling a spot, there are always appropriate times to perform the diverse music available; they are yours to find.

Be cautious of dismissing all pop music out of hand. The educational concepts of arched phrasing, proper breathing, formation of vowels, and diction are just as important in pop music as in classical music. Be sure to point this out and show specific examples of how the two are related. Make the most of a diverse program—always remember to guide your students to transfer musical style from one genre to another.

In the pursuit of a balanced program you should consider the enjoyment of your audience. Even though you have taken the time to educate your audience about classical music, let's say, it's not fair to your audience or your singers to be so one dimensional. Having a variety of music for your audience is most certainly a recipe for success.

Finding music

There are many ways to find new pieces of music:

- Attend reading sessions at conventions, workshops or in-services. Let selection criteria, like your choir students' ability and programming needs, be your guide. This will help prevent you from selecting music just because you like it.

- Attend concerts of other middle schools and high schools in your area.

- Read choral publishers' catalogs and promotions. Order music on approval if necessary.

Another effective way to expose yourself to new music and help select it is to develop a network of fellow choral educators with whom to share music and ideas. This collaboration will help you learn what works for your fellow directors and their students, and by extension, what might work for you and your students. You will not only broaden your horizons to include different types of choral music, but you will discover ideas to help you develop your musicianship and make your choral program more educational, fun and exciting. You will also share and learn new ways to perform or present the music in a concert setting.

Every choral performance, from concerts, festivals and conventions to church services, reflects the director's selection of music. Some performances are all show and pop; others are all classical. Some are upbeat and uplifting; others ask you to think and better understand the world. In spite of this musical diversity, if you see and hear the choir's musical sincerity in their performance, it is by no means an accident!

If directors take the time to select appropriate music and share even a small part of their decision-making process with the group, it will go along to securing a "buy in" from the choir members. Directors are often asked how they are able to get their choirs "into" singing classical music, performing it with total fulfillment and enjoyment and giving it the musical treatment it demands. The answer is simple—it depends on the director's initial presentation. This really makes a difference!

From my perspective...

by Linda Spevacek

A dartboard...52 pickup...while both are technically options for selecting music, neither will result in the successful program you are working towards. Here are a few that will, specific to the level of the ensemble:

High School choirs:

- Early in the year, select music that builds confidence, especially in the male sections.

- If you are short on tenors (or are trying to build confidence), consider repertoire in the SSAB voicing. Most programs have enough women to divide into three parts, which allows for a four-part sound. Encourage dealers to separate the SSAB voicing from the SAB. When asked at workshops or reading sessions what you'd like to have, say SSAB.

- Offer students a carrot. Entice them to rise to a higher level by the end of the semester with a difficult arrangement or masterwork. Tell them your short- and long-term musical and technical goals. Believe it or not, they want to know the plan of your collective musical journey and be a part of it.

Middle School/Junior High choirs:

- See above if you have SATB choirs.
- If using three-part music, select a few familiar tunes that are arranged—spirituals, folk tunes, or Broadway or pop music. If using the latter, select choral melodies that allow you to work with the group's tone and blend and/or Face Factor.[11]
- End the rehearsal with a light, fun piece.

Elementary choirs:

- Begin the year with unison pieces and rounds.
- Select two-part songs that can be taught first in unison, adding parts as students' ears become stronger and independence begins to happen.
- Familiar songs such as folk songs or spirituals are good choices for this level too. If considering a Broadway or popular tune, look for depth, places to teach technique, phrasing, etc.
- Give them a "teaser" piece that is more difficult. Choose one with a foreign language or one by a classical composer and tell them once they are a little more experienced, you can't wait to let them see how well they will do with it!

Select quality music in all styles.

- Respect students enough to offer them sophisticated music and they will respond accordingly.
- Use energetic songs at first, or rhythmic songs to which you may later add body movement.
- Songs with a speech chorus are an immediate success for even non-singers.

Continued...

[11] See page 95 to learn about the Face Factor.

- Folk songs with familiar melodies also work well.
- Those songs with texts of well-known poets are great, as they promote discussion and students can relate the poetry to their other subjects.
- Classical songs are wonderful for similar reasons. You can discuss the composer's life and the students can get extra credit for writing a report and sharing it with the class.

In all cases, ask yourself:

- Does it have a shape, an apex? A good piece of music has proportion.
- Does it make a statement?
- Does it make you and the choir members feel sadness, joy, adoration, love, anger, silly…something? The pieces will change but you will never forget the feelings you had while singing them.

Part Four

Notes, Quotes, Jokes, Qs & As

16 FAQs: Answers to Frequently Asked Questions

There seem to be universal questions asked by everyone involved with chorus—teachers, students, parents, and administrators. The following are some of these frequently asked questions along with answers that provide suggestions on how to best address the questions.

Q. What if someone confronts me because I am teaching choral music with a religious or sacred overtone?

A. First, you may want to use the word "sacred" as opposed to "religious." Not only is it the more accurate term for describing non-secular works, it's broader in nature and may feel less personally directed. Then, explain that you are not teaching religion, but exposing the students to beautiful music written hundreds of years ago that happened to be sung with a sacred text. You may reinforce your position with the 1967 ruling of the United States Supreme Court that permits the study of any music that doesn't advance or inhibit religion:

> *Sacred music...may be included in the curriculum, as long as it's presented in a prudent and objective manner. For instance, the study of art history would be incomplete without the study of the Sistine Chapel, and the study of architecture requires the study of Renaissance Cathedrals. If it's possible to study Communism without indoctrination, then it must be possible to study sacred music without parochialistic attitudes and sectarian points of view.*

Q. Why do choruses sing in foreign languages? Why not just sing in English so we can all understand it?

A. From a purely technical perspective, singing in foreign languages gives us a learning tool to focus on proper vowel sounds. Beyond that, studying music from different countries and cultures exercises the mind and helps us broaden our educational horizons. It provides a springboard for a discussion about the composer's native country or the time period in which a piece was composed, in the case of texts in a classical language, such as Latin. And while choir and audience members alike may not fully understand the text, the use of a foreign language adds a mystical beauty and character to the music, thereby diversifying the concert. Last but not least, the text presented is what the composer had in mind for the final musical performance. Can you imagine "Taps" being played on a flute?

Q. Why are we required to attend concerts?

A. Attendance requirements help us learn to be responsible. As President Reagan famously said, "90 percent of life is just showing up." In any job, you must attend and perform your work in order to get paid. If you make a commitment to a sports team, music ensemble or any group, you also make a commitment to attend the games, concerts or meetings.

Q. How do we work with special needs students when we are not properly trained to do so?

A. Working with special needs students presents a unique set of challenges. Consider telling the administration that you would rather not know which students are classified "special needs" and which are not. Removing your own potential for bias will help you keep all students on a more level playing field when teaching. If you identify students who are struggling with even the most basic choral part, step up to the challenge and find a way to include them in choir. You may ask the students to be the audience and see how they liked the choir's singing. You may assign simple tasks or even give them a hand drum (even if it's off beat). Obviously, each case is different from the next, so you must use your best judgment. Do not be afraid to seek the advice of the special education facilitator or the student's primary classroom teacher. (It should go without saying that even if a placement was made without your approval, your frustration with the counselor or administrator should never be taken out on a student.)

Q. What if our class is treated as a "dumping ground"?

A. There are several ways to handle this common complaint from choral educators:

- *Communicate with the counselor or registrar about your choral program.* While making it clear that you understand that the whole school doesn't operate around your choral program, outline your goals for the choral program.

- *Consider a compromise.* You will open a non-auditioned music/choral class that is open to all students in exchange for discretion over placement in auditioned choirs. Remember, you can't have everything and you must always be willing to compromise.

- *Keep an open mind.* Sometimes the student who appears to be the worst problem may turn out to be your most loyal, hardest-working student.

- *Be organized and easy to work with.* If you have things up and running with a great deal of success, those in charge of scheduling your classes will be more willing to listen to your needs and work with you.

Q. How do we work with the non-English-speaking students?

A. Instead of seeing the students as a hindrance, think of a choral music education as the best way for them to learn the English language. If the class is reacting with disrespect, you have the unique opportunity to put them in these students' shoes every time you have to learn a song in a foreign language.

Q. What are ways we can communicate what we do to the school administration, teachers and staff?

A. Communication can begin with something as simple as, "Do you have a few minutes to talk?" You could initiate communication with a note, card, e-mail, etc. Any initial communication should begin with something positive, such as, "You have to come into the chorus room and see what great things are happening." Administrators and classroom teachers like to feel informed and not left out of the loop. If you have something going on, let them know. However, always understand that the administrators have a great deal on their minds in the overall operation of the school, so make sure any communication is concise and to the point.

Q. What if I have no money in the chorus budget?

A. It's up to you to seek out the money that is available for your classes. If these classes are part of the school's schedule, there is operational money. Ask administrators. Be persistent. Consider other sources and be creative. Many districts have textbook funds; try to apply those dollars to collections. The choral library is a library; work to gain access to a portion of those funds. If you are unable to secure funds, you will likely have to explore fundraisers.

Q. How do I work with the school's scheduling?

A. Be flexible and use any unique scheduling anomalies to your advantage. If you have longer classes on certain days, plan special, extended lessons on theory, history, leadership skills, etc., or bring in a guest speaker. Plan activities for shorter classes too. Theory worksheets, aural examples, even listening can all be adjusted to work in nearly any class period. If you stay positive, you will find that you will be able to work things out and get things done no matter what schedule is thrown at you.

Q. How do I get my parents involved with my students' progress, or even with my choral program?

A. Most chorus teachers are Type A personalities. We are perfectionists who take our jobs very seriously and want to get everything done on our own. Given this pressure we put on ourselves to succeed, it's only natural to want to do everything we can to get the job done right. There will come a time, however, when your choral program becomes large and takes on a life of its own and there *will* be too many things for any one person to do. You must get parents involved in your program before that time comes.

Task students with creating a monthly newsletter or a website to keep your parents informed of what is going on with the choral program. Send personal notes or letters inviting parents to come and hear the choir at any opportunity. Offer parents the opportunity to help with tasks. Mainly, keep yourself unobstructed and keep an open door to anyone willing to get involved with your program.

Q. How do I get my audience to display proper concert etiquette during our concerts?

A. Print a concert etiquette paragraph in your program. Train your students to show the utmost display of etiquette while other choirs are performing. Keep your concerts efficient with their stage deportment. But mostly, if you put out a good product, people will buy it with very little interference.

Q. What if my administrators do not understand or appreciate my choral program or, worse yet, think it's unimportant?

A. It's up to you to put your best foot forward. Invite your administrators to see and hear what you are doing. If you did your homework, they will have no choice but to appreciate your work and your contribution to the school. However, always remember that you are only a part of the school's overall educational program. If you appreciate the balancing act that your administrators have to do, they will appreciate you and feel your choral program is important. Remember that respect from anyone has to be earned, especially when that person has a position that is, on paper at least, higher than yours.

Q. How should my students stand?

A. This could also be asked, "what do the singers do with their hands?" Instruct your singers to touch their fingertips to the side seams of their pants or dresses and not to remove their hands. If they have an itch, it will go away. No matter what, students should never touch their faces. Girls with long hair and those who like to flip their hair should wear it back in barrettes.

Once you have a clear plan for how your students are going to stand, practice this until all students are situated to your satisfaction. Then, tell your students to remember this arrangement and keep a picture of their stance, placement and position in their minds.

Q. How do I keep my choir students from passing out on stage?

A. It's "locking the knees" which causes one to pass out. To counter this tendency, many singers are told to "bend their knees," but this overreaction can easily result in an unnecessarily awkward-looking choir. We are able to stand up straight and keep blood flowing freely. Rather, it's the locking or "squeezing" of the knees that must be avoided. One much less distracting technique is to have singers "wiggle their toes" to keep the blood circulating.

Anticipation: A Key to Sustaining Success

Linda Spevacek

Anticipate...possible chaos

It's first day of school. You have no idea what kinds of attitudes your students will have in each of the classes. What can you do to start the year off on the right foot? Before chaos occurs, visualize a successful first day, over and over. Visualize the atmosphere of your ideal classroom and the attitudes of your students. Visualize your attitude, your body language and your command of the situation. Even if you have doubts as to your ability to control, you must act as though you do not. What you act, you become.

Have a quote posted on the board that sets the tone and helps define your expectations. Consider one about winners. Reinforce the concept that when students are in your class, they will be winners.

Anticipate...negativity

A few respected teachers in your school will not support your program.

This will stem from everything from bad past experiences with music to a desire for power and control. Set out to win them over. Be friendly. Learn their interests and find a way to include them in your choral program. Consider asking them to read a text before a song or assist with the audio-visual elements of the program. Invite a few teachers over for an informal barbeque. Work to break down barriers to music instead of building them up.

Anticipate...a budget cut

Have optional fundraisers in the back of your mind. Ask parents and students to brainstorm fundraising opportunities and cost-cutting measures. Make yourself a vital part of the community so that the parents, school board members, and local businesses and organizations will be affected by the cut in your programs.

Get out in the community. Take a few talented students to sing for the Lions Club. Take a quartet of girls to sing at the country club. Present a solo or small group from the upcoming musical at a Rotary meeting or other business organization luncheon. Show off your best often and word will travel fast. Then, if need be, these organizations may be asked to write letters on your behalf or to make a donation to the music and/or choir fund.

Anticipate...by asking "what if?"

Your upcoming concert is vital to building your program and showing your administration your organizational skills. You are stressed because there are too many details and too little time for you to make sure the performance comes off without a hitch.

Ask yourself, what if there is not a music stand with music on it when the curtain opens? What if the microphones have static? What if the sound guy is sick that evening? Now, plan for the what ifs.

Have I checked with the stagehand about placing the music stand and music? Is there a backup sound engineer? Do I have extra copies of music? Do I know whom to thank? Have I planned what I am going to say about certain pieces? Delegate various details to responsible students; meet after school once a week for ten minutes to lock everything in.

Anticipate...musical and technical difficulties

You are presenting a new piece of music that is out of your students' present realm of capabilities. What if they can't feel the rhythm? Do you have short drills or body movements planned for success? What if the range stretches them a bit more than before? Do you have technical suggestions and immediate fixes to help them successfully execute the new notes? What if they sing the incorrect vowels? Are you prepared to help them? What if the piece is in a new style? Have you collected interesting background information that students will relate to to help them get excited about experiencing the new style? Can you relate it to architecture or poetry of the period?

Teach the students to anticipate in class. How am I going to sing that phrase? How do I want to feel while singing this piece? What vowel do I sing? What vocal technique do I use? How much breath pressure should I sing with? And what resonator shapes? To what extent should I open or work with those shapes to create the sound I want? Is my concert attire clean? Pressed? Do I have the right shoes? The sooner young people learn to ask themselves "What if?" the sooner they will be able to make choices based on their desired outcome.

Winners vs. Losers: Attitude Is Everything

18

The act of taking the first step is what separates the winners from the losers.

—Brian Tracy

A baby taking its first step seems to bring so much joy to everyone—parents, siblings, grandparents, and anyone anxious to watch this momentous event. When we were babies, we probably would have just as soon as crawled forever. It took our parents to guide us and encourage us into taking our first step—an event so momentus that we refer to taking any chance in life as "taking the first step."

Although we have people in our youth to encourage us, the older we get, the more it's up to us to take our own first steps. If you have the guts to take the first step with anything you are trying to achieve, the next step is a little easier and the next few steps much easier, until it becomes effortless. Do not be afraid to take the first step in anything you want to accomplish!

Whenever you see a successful business, someone once made a courageous decision.

—Peter Drucker

Most of the people who see the final choral product on the stage have no idea the steps and courage it took along the way. If you are waiting for them to, you will wait forever. Like any program, sport or business, you can never totally understand what it takes to make it successful unless you actually do it. Instead of seeing this as a negative, use it as a catalyst to make courageous decisions! Just as people may not understand your effort and courage in making decisions, they will also not understand your failures when things don't work out the way you may have liked. Just go for it! Ultimately, you have nothing to lose!

Always do more than is required of you.

—George S. Patton

Winners always find ways to go above and beyond what is expected of them. Losers always find ways to get out of work, and in the process usually spend more time than the task itself would have taken. When you do more than is required of you, you always strengthen yourself and others around you!

If everyone is thinking alike, then somebody isn't thinking.

—George S. Patton

Winners always express their way of thinking, even if it goes against what everyone else is thinking. They will also be quick to know if their way of thinking will not work or will not benefit a project. Losers will always be quick to nod their heads and jump on to someone else's thought, even if they don't fully understand it. Do not fall into this trap. Offer what you have on your mind and bring it up for discussion. Trust yourself!

Associate yourself with men of good quality if you esteem your own reputation, for 'tis better to be alone than in bad company.

—George Washington

If you are thinking like a winner, you will have a tendency to surround yourself with winners. You will work well with these people to get great things done. If you think positively, others usually have no choice but to think positively, and as always results from positive thinking, great things will happen. On the other hand, losers tend to bolster the adage that misery loves company. They stick together, get little accomplished and think negatively. It will come as no surprise that most of the time, their prophecy comes true (making them strangely and temporarily happy). Even if you have to stick it out alone for a while, never give in to negative people with negative energy.

From my perspective...

by Linda Spevacek

You can help create a class of winners simply by your own attitude. If you see yourself as a winner, you will portray a winning attitude to your students or have that winning attitude reflected in your students. If you don't believe you are a winner, ask yourself what would it take to make yourself feel that way. Do what it takes to see yourself as a winner.

Collect sayings about winners.
Post them at home and in your choir and music rooms.
Believe them.[12]

The Winner is always part of the answer.
The Loser is always a part of the problem.
The Winner always has a program.
The Loser always has an excuse.
The Winner says, "Let me do it for you."
The Loser says, "That's not my job."
The Winner sees an answer for every problem.
The Loser sees a problem for every answer.
The Winner sees a green near every sand trap.
The Loser sees two or three sand traps near every green.
The Winner says, "It may be difficult but it's possible."
The Loser says, "It may be possible but it's too difficult."
The Winner goes the extra mile, knowing it's never crowded.
The Loser never starts.

Continued...

[12] A marvelous book on the power of attitudes is *Attitudes Are Contagious... Are Yours Worth Catching?* by Dennis E. Mannering, published by Options Unlimited, Inc. Visit www.mannerings.com for more information.

The Winner decides to do things.
    The Loser has to do things.
The Winner makes it happen.
    The Loser lets it happen.

Winners never whine.

Winners are losers who gave it a little more time.

Winners aren't created, they create themselves.

19

Wisdom of the Ages: Famous Quotes as They Pertain to Teaching

Utilizing famous quotations from famous people is a fun and exciting sponge activity and an excellent way to close rehearsal. A quote of the day gives the students a chance to focus on their own intellectual side and is a way for them to transfer previously learned material to other subject areas.

When you read a quote to your students, allow them the latitude to offer their insight—they will pleasantly surprise you when they share their point of view! Often, a student will shed new light on a statement, new light that may have never occurred to you. Once a dialog has been opened, have the students share with each other how this quote will affect them, or how they can use it in or apply it to everyday life. When reciting and discussing the quote, you may offer your own thoughts as to how it pertains to teaching. You may also share with students how this quote applies to your own everyday life in an effort to spark discussion.

Every time you come across a quote, any quote, which strikes a chord with you, write it down and share it with your students. Once you become familiar with famous quotes, you will find yourself saying a few of your favorites over and over. Upon each hearing, the students will better understand your motivation and they will have a tool to latch on to while they are learning.

The price of greatness is responsibility.

—Winston Churchill

Often, it's hard to convince students to get a job done right because they soon learn that they can cut corners and probably get the same grade. Use this quote to turn that attitude around. Tell your students that if they want to be great at something, they must take on the responsibility. Responsibility can mean showing up on time, going the extra mile when writing a paper or doing a project, or attending extra rehearsals if for no other reason than to help other students. Once students understand that with the greatness they possess comes a responsibility for the good of other people, they will feel good about what they are doing and help many people in the process.

This is a lesson we choral educators could benefit from revisiting now and then, too. As "jacks of all trades" *and* masters of many, it's easy to feel that our skills are being abused and that we are being taken for granted. Instead of embracing this attitude, discover a new outlook on your life by accepting that with great abilities come great responsibilities. How many of us were great the first day we walked into the classroom? Rather, we became great because along the way many people mentored us. We picked up new ideas and better ways of getting things done, and we learned how to run things more smoothly and efficiently. Our responsibility now is to help others along this same way. It feels good when we help someone else save time!

Eating words has never given me indigestion.

—Winston Churchill

How many times have we lie awake all night thinking about something we said to our students, and wishing we wouldn't have said it? We are all guilty of saying something they we shouldn't have, but if we can eat what we say before we say it, it will probably be best for everyone involved in the long run.

Teachers need to have a quick "mental snap" if they are to easily convince their students that it's not good to say bad things about other people. Students need to be told that what they say to their neighbors will last forever and can never be taken back once it's spoken. However, if they refrain from saying something nasty to their neighbor—that is, just "eat your words," the nasty thought will eventually go away.

Far and away the best prize that life offers is the chance to work hard at work worth doing.

—Theodore Roosevelt

Working with children who are going through adolescence is a somewhat common task that everyone has engaged in at some point in time. But "working with" is something entirely different from the specialized task that secondary teachers have. This is particularly true in the case of chorus teachers, who have the additional task of working with the voice at a time when it can be at its most vulnerable. If we are able to take these children and have them sing and live in harmony—that is work worth doing! Let's take it upon ourselves to take pride in what we do and work as hard as we can in doing what we love to do!

Adolescence is the age where students are beginning to think seriously about what career they may want to pursue. Of course, we all have only one life to live, so let's shoot for the top—having a job we can love! Oftentimes, how much a job pays is the first criteria for choosing a job. However, once your paycheck is established, you must spend within its portion, which leaves you with the quality of your job and its satisfaction. If you choose a career that you feel is worth doing, you will automatically work hard at it!

You aren't really wealthy until you have something money can't buy.

—Garth Brooks

In this busy, busy world, it's sometimes hard to put things into perspective. It took weeks to deliver the Declaration of Independence from the American Colonies to England, yet today if the day's lunch order is improperly faxed to a restaurant, it can ruin everyone's day. Years ago, it took weeks and weeks to travel across the country, yet now if our plane is delayed an hour or so, it can spark a major-league shouting match in a terminal. Whereas our grandparents would get their news once a week on a newsreel in the movie theater, we get our news as it happens on our PC.

Nobody can deny how these wonderful conveniences have made life easier at times, but somewhere, lost in the shuffle, are two facts: 1) having and enjoying them changed the way we live and 2) they cost money. Attaining these modern luxuries usually requires both parents to work, and sometimes our students get lost in the same shuffle. It can seem as though money makes the world go around, but does it really?

Blessed is he that expects nothing, for he shall never be disappointed.

—Benjamin Franklin

Teachers will most likely never become millionaires from their professions. Get over that! Whining about your salary will not make it increase. Instead, rejoice in all of the satisfying and rewarding things about the teaching profession, all of which cost us nothing. Many people in other fields envy how much we enjoy our profession. In the long run, to love your job and look forward to going to "work" every day is worth more than anything a million dollars could possibly buy.

If a man hasn't discovered something that he will die for, he isn't fit to live.

—Martin Luther King, Jr.

You should feel extremely strong and proud about your position as a teacher, a chorus director, a counselor, a mentor, and a role model. The prouder you are about your position, the more effective you will be in your classroom and with your students.

The best leader is the one who has sense enough to pick good people to do what he wants done, and self-restraint enough to keep from meddling with them while they do it.

—Theodore Roosevelt

As chorus teachers, we often have the privilege of choosing the students we want to be in our classes. Most of the time, we audition the students. Other times, we are our own feeder program. Of course, there are times when a computer, a counselor, an eager parent, or an administrator chooses students for you, but for the most part, once you get your program going, you choose most of your students.

Once those students are in your classroom, we often have a tendency to want to control everything that the students do—we choose the music, we tell them what voice part they should sing, we style the music exactly the way we want it to be. Put yourself in their shoes—would you like an administrator to tell you exactly how to teach? Would you like your entire program to be decided at a parents' meeting?

Encourage students to get involved, to take the initiative to contribute to *their* program. Students can help recruit, help clean the room, help design the program, help with selecting music, help with choralography, and especially, help correct their own mistakes during a rehearsal. Most of the time, the choral singers easily detect a mistake they made, either as an individual or collectively as a group. Before you say anything, back up a few measures, sing the passage again and just see what happens. The chorus students just may surprise you!

To know what is right and not to do it is the worst cowardice.

—Confucius

One thing that separates music teachers from other teachers is that we must be able to thrive under pressure and put our work on public display. Music teachers work with many students, parents and supporters and we will never have the ability to please everyone all of the time. Whenever we make any decision, we must know that someone will always criticize, no matter how successful and fruitful the decision becomes. So make a decision and move on. Others will move on as well, even those who did not like or agree with your decision in the first place.

Winning is not a sometime thing; it's an all-the-time thing.

—Vince Lombardi

When your classroom procedures are well planned and an established part of your routine, go over them often. When you have classroom rules and procedures, they should be an integral part of your classroom management or choral rehearsal, not just rules for the sake of having rules. If your procedures are what makes a winning situation in your room, keep on top of them all of the time. Everyone needs reminders; don't be afraid of repetition when it comes to classroom rules and procedures.

Failure is only the opportunity to begin again more intelligently.

—Henry Ford

We all make mistakes. We will all continue to make mistakes. That's fine. What isn't fine is making mistakes and failing to learn from them. Making mistakes is one of the easiest ways to learn; don't miss that opportunity. And when you capitalize on those opportunities, keep the lesson learned fresh in your mind and on guard for any situation.

When you're green, you're growing; and when you're ripe, you start to rot.

—Ray Kroc

Most of us absolutely love what we do, but there are times we feel as though we are about to rot. (And if we feel this way, imagine how our students must feel when our teaching methods remain the same day after day!) If you feel tired with your job, you must either find new and exciting methods, surroundings, music, people, etc., or find a new job altogether. Always explore new and exciting ways to keep yourself, and well as your students, green and growing!

I'm a great believer of luck, and I find the harder I work the more I have of it.

—Thomas Jefferson

People often wish they could do this and want to have that, yet have no real substance to help back up their ambitions or aspirations. No matter what the field is—sports, music, business, education, or parenting—it's hard work that makes the difference. Some people are blessed with great minds, athletic skills, good looks, or great wealth. However, what separates average people from superior people is how they take their skills and work to develop them. You cannot control luck, but you can control your work ethic. Successful people may be accused of having luck attached to their success, but their accusers are usually those who always wished to make things happen but never really put in the effort.

The world cares very little about what one knows; it's what one is able to do that counts.

—Booker T. Washington

The time you spend thinking that you know everything there is to know about your profession is time you spend cheating yourself, and those who surround you, of knowledge. Never be too proud to expose your inexperience or lack of knowledge. Seeking advice on how to better improve any situation is a good thing. We all came into this world not knowing anything, yet along the way we learned a great deal from those around us. Do not feel like a fool if you want or need to gain knowledge.

On speech making: "Be sincere, be brief, be seated."

—Franklin D. Roosevelt

When it comes to concert programming, direct teaching or actually speaking in front of a group, "be sincere, be brief, be seated." The longer the speech, the greater chance for those listening to become bored. Additionally, teachers must make every attempt to talk as little as possible and let the students generate the teaching and learning.

A place where optimism flourishes most is in the lunatic asylum.

—Havelock Ellis

If you have a license for humor in your room, you are definitely expanding your options to promote success. Defuse tense situations—be it a student challenging a classroom rule or a direction given from the teacher—with humor. It doesn't have to be a laugh-out-loud joke, but a humorous, non-threatening response can go along way. If a student has initiated a humorous moment, even if it is at your expense, don't be too quick to stifle it. It may allow you to connect with the student and ultimately earn his or her respect, or it may allow you an opportunity to quickly make your point without escalating the situation and causing further disruption in your class. Indeed, humor in the classroom can be a powerful tool in teaching. The students will appreciate your understanding and will usually respond with better behavior as a reward to your understanding and ability to lighten up and add humor to a situation.

Try not to become a man of success but rather try to become a man of value.

—Albert Einstein

As chorus teachers, we are often striving for excellence and driven to achieve at a high level. Our success is often measured by the quality of a performance, which makes some sense. This is, after all, what the public sees and hears. However, it's up to us to keep thriving to become people of value, and we certainly know what that is. Day after day, we do many things of great value to help our students become better people, which, most of the time, go unnoticed. Still, if we use value as a barometer of our success, society will be much better off in the long run because of our daily efforts.

You can make more friends in two months by becoming interested in other people than you can in two years by trying to get other people interested in you.

—Dale Carnegie

This is especially true when you are recruiting new students. If you take an interest in them, they will have no choice but to want to be a part of your program. They will sense that you are a terrific person to work with because you took an interest in them as a person. It will be self-evident that you are a person who takes no less interest in your choral program.

This is also true when you are dealing with administrators, colleagues, parents, and supporters. The harder you try to toot your program's horn, the less interested they will become. However, if you take an interest in the point of view of others, they will naturally take an interest in what you are doing. They will also take a greater, more long-lasting interest because they initiated it.

Don't measure yourself by what you have accomplished, but by what you should have accomplished with your ability.

—John Wooden

You are the only one who truly knows what you are made of. You are the only one who truly knows if you are using your abilities to your best advantage, and for the benefit of others and the society as a whole. When you take on life with all of your abilities, great things will happen!

More of Randy and Linda's favorite quotes

Don't let the negative few outweigh the positive many.

—Anon.

Many a problem will solve itself if you forget it and go fishing.

—Olin Miller

The biggest problem in the world could have been solved when it was small.

—Anon.

Whenever you're wrong, admit it; whenever you're right, shut up.

—Ogden Nash

Train your students to learn to listen, and in a way they listen to learn.

—*Anon.*

The true greats I have ever known in my life all had one thing in common. They had great energy and focused that energy on one thing at a time.

—*Charlton Heston*

We are what we repeatedly do. Excellence, then, is not an act, but a habit.

—*Aristotle*

I don't think much of a man who is not wiser than he was yesterday.

—*Abraham Lincoln*

You never achieve real success unless you like what you are doing.

—*Dale Carnegie*

Formal education will make you a living; self-education will make you a fortune.

—*Jim Rohn*

Character cannot be developed in ease and quiet. Only through experience of trial and suffering can the soul be strengthened, ambition inspired and success achieved.

—*Helen Keller*

Manners are a sensitive awareness of the feelings of others.

—*Emily Post*

Am I not destroying my enemies by making friends of them?

—*Abraham Lincoln*

Wise men don't need advice. Fools won't take it.

—*Benjamin Franklin*

In any moment of decision the best thing you can do is the right thing, the next best thing is the wrong thing, and the worst thing you can do is nothing.

—*Theodore Roosevelt*

One man with courage makes a majority.

—*Andrew Jackson*

If you want to succeed, you should strike out on new paths rather than travel the worn paths of accepted success.

—*John D. Rockefeller, Jr.*

Nearly all men can stand adversity, but if you want to test a man's character, give him power.

—*Abraham Lincoln*

Who is rich? He that rejoices in his portion.

—*Benjamin Franklin*

Leadership is the art of getting someone else to do something you want done because he wants to do it.

—*Dwight D. Eisenhower*

A Good Teacher

Now, therefore, the superior teacher leads his students and doesn't pull them along. He urges them to go forward and doesn't suppress them. He opens the way to them, but he doesn't take them to the place.

Leading without pulling makes the process of learning gentle. Urging without suppressing makes the process of learning easy, and opening the way to the students without taking them to the place makes them think for themselves.

Now, if the process of education is made gentle and easy and if the students are taught to think for themselves, we may call the man a good teacher.

—*Confucius*

Only A Teacher

I am a teacher! What I do and say is absorbed by young minds who will echo these images across the ages. My lessons will be immortal, affecting people yet unborn, people I will never see or know. The future of the world is in my classroom today and this future has potential for both good or bad. The pliable minds of tomorrow's leaders will be molded either artistically or grotesquely by what I do.

Several future presidents are learning from me today; so are the great writers of the next decades and so are all the so-called ordinary people who will make the decisions in a democracy.

Only a teacher? Thank God I have a calling to the greatest profession of all! I must be vigilant everyday lest I lose one fragile opportunity to improve tomorrow.

—*Dr. Ivan Fitzwater*

He Who Laughs, Last: Humor in the Classroom

Linda Spevacek

Choral educators are always under pressure to produce. Not only are their programs visible to the administration and the community, many directors lean towards perfectionism. The combination of the external pressure of concerts and parents' meetings and the internal drive to always perform and be "the best" creates a high level of stress. This leads many directors to burn out or experience exhaustion. This stress level is not improved by following old adages like, "never smile before Thanksgiving." Instead, research from the past few years indicates that adding laughter and humor to our lives will result in happier, healthier people of all ages.

Laughter is life's greatest lubricant.

—Art Linkletter

The idea that laughter can be therapeutic certainly isn't a new one—the Bible says, "a merry heart doeth good like a medicine"—but recent research has been extensive. In his book, *The Doctors' Guide to Instant Stress Relief,* Dr. Ronald G. Nathan says:

> Laughter can release stress from the body as well as lighten stressful situations. Some call it 'internal jogging' because it increases your heart rate, breathing activity, blood pressure, body temperature, and natural pain-killing chemicals. Muscles tense as we wait

> for the punch line, contract as we laugh, and relax profoundly—for up to forty-five minutes—as we recover from the excitement of laughing. Heart rate and blood pressure then drop below pre-laugh levels.

Dr. Nathan also pointed to other studies that suggest laughter creates a stronger immune system and is nearly as effective in reducing stress as biofeedback training. Another noted physician and Stanford University professor has reported similar curative effects of laughter, pointing out that as well as soothing an aching heart, it's good exercise and is mentally and physically stimulating.

The physiological effects are many: when you laugh, the thorax, chest and abdominal muscles contract. A hearty belly laugh may cause your systolic blood pressure to rise from an average of 120 to 200, and can double your pulse rate from 60 to 120 beats per minute. It also pumps extra adrenalin into the blood stream, which may stimulate endorphin production—the body's painkiller—to the brain. Laughter creates a feeling of euphoria and results in lowered levels of stress, hypertension and muscle-tension headaches. A thought to consider in our nation's constant battle against teen drug use: inducing a natural euphoria with humor and laughter could minimize the demand for a drug-induced euphoria.

Another interesting study actually began in the entertainment industry. While watching audiences laugh, television executive Sherry Dunay Hilber often wondered about the physical and emotional effects of all that chuckling and chortling. She took her questions to UCLA doctors, including Lonnie Zeltzer, director of UCLA's pediatric pain program. Zeltzer's team hammered out a plan for an innovative study called "Rx Laughter" at UCLA's Jonsson Cancer Center. A major goal of their research is to determine if laughter lessens the pain of kids with cancer and other chronic pain problems.

So far, the project has unearthed some interesting results. Zeltzer's team found that healthy children were able to keep their arms in frigid ice water for a longer period of time if they were watching funny videos. The kids also reported less pain and had lower levels of stress hormones. "I think humor is a way of helping the body's natural pain-control system work better at the level of neurotransmitters, like endorphins and other chemicals," Zeltzer said.

Make humor a habit in your classroom

Adopt a childlike perspective. Whenever you feel tense, ask yourself, "How would a nine-year-old see this situation?"

It has been said that people laugh fifteen times a day. Do you? Do your students? If not, look for humor. Surround yourself with people or things that bring humor into your daily life. Try out-of-the-ordinary repertoire that is humorous, silly or just plain fun (a list appears below).

Incorporate "humor therapy" moments in your class. Set aside time each day to focus on something funny, whether it's a piece of music or a comical situation. Remember, if you cannot laugh at yourself, there are plenty of students who will do it for you. Have a joke of the week on the board. Post a musical cartoon. Tell a quick joke about sopranos, altos, tenors, basses, and most importantly, conductors. It's great to get the students involved, as it builds camaraderie and a healthy teasing among the sections, but remember that adolescence is a delicate time and feelings must be carefully guarded.

Out-of-the-Ordinary Repertoire[13]

"Antonio," by Eugene Butler
Two-part

"Boomwhacker® Boogie," by George L.O. Strid and Mary Donnelly
Two-part

"Braces Blues," by Phyllis Wolfe White
Unison/Two-part

"Breathing With Beethoven," by Phyllis Wolfe White
Three-part Mixed; Unison/Two-part

"Bus Stop (Can't Be Late!)," by Phyllis Wolfe White
Unison/Two-part

"Christmas…in about Three Minutes," by Mark Weston
SATB; SSA; TB; Three-part Mixed; Two-part

"Christmas Is Coming and We Are Getting Fat," by Dave and Jean Perry
Two-part

Continued…

[13] All titles are published by Heritage Music Press and are available from your favorite music supplier. Visit www.lorenz.com for audio samples of most of these titles.

"Classical Boomwhackers®," by Brad Printz
Unison

"Chumbara," by Dave and Jean Perry
Two-part

"The Copyscat Rag," by Linda Spevacek
Two-part

"Eine Kleine Spufmusik," by Linda Spevacek
Three-part Mixed

"The Entertainer Ragtime Cowboy Joe," by Linda Spevacek
Three-part Mixed; Two-part

"Flops of the Fifties," by Stephen Lawrence
SATB

"Folk Song Nonsense," by Greg Gilpin
Two-part

"A Hamburger and an Order of Flies," by Stephen Lawrence
Three-part mixed; Two-part ACV

"A Holiday Hand Jive," by Greg Gilpin
Three-part Mixed; Two-part

"Holiday Tango," by Linda Spevacek
SATB

"I Love Chocolate," by Mary Lynn Lightfoot
Unison/Two-part

"In My Closet," by Phyllis Wolfe White
Two-part

"It's In My Desk," by Mary Lynn Lightfoot
Two-part

"It's Ruff Being a Dog," by Phyllis Wolfe White and Marta Keen
Two-part

"I've Lost My Homework," by Marta Keen
Two-part

"Jabberwocky," by Boyd Bacon
SATB

"Ja-Da," by Linda Spevacek
Two-part; Three-part Mixed

"Jingle All the Ways," by Brad Printz
Three-part Mixed

"Jingle Bells Through the Ages," by Allen Pote
SATB; SSA; Three-part Mixed; Two-part

"The Kid with the Surprising Sneeze," by Bill Vollinger
Two-part

"Mistletoe," by Phyllis Wolfe White
Three-part Mixed; Two-part

"Mozart's Messy Room Sonata," by Phyllis Wolfe White
Three-part Mixed; Two-part

"Musical Memories," by Dave and Jean Perry
Three-part Mixed/SATB; Two-part

"The Not-So-Boring Minuet," by Phyllis Wolfe White
Three-part Mixed; Unison

"The Nuttycracker Suite," by Linda Spevacek
Two-part

"Painless Opera," by Phyllis Wolfe White
Three-part Mixed; Unison

"Plain Cheeseburger," by Phyllis Wolfe White
Two-part

"Polly Wolly Doodle," by Brad Printz
SAB; Two-part

"Pop Bottle Hoedown," by Linda Spevacek
Two-part

"Santa's Going on a Diet," by Stephen Lawrence
Two-part

"Seein' Things at Night," by Jan Reese
Two-part

"Shake It Up Shakespeare," by Phyllis Wolfe White
Three-part Mixed

"Shh!," by Vijay Singh
Four-part speech choir

"Spoof à la Classique," by Linda Spevacek
Three-part Mixed

"Three Creature Features," by Dave and Jean Perry
Two-part

"Three Fragmented Farces: In the Style of the English Madrigal," by Gary Walth
SATB

"Three Little Pigs: A Howling Success Story," by Stephen Lawrence
Unison

"Tiger Rag," by Linda Spevacek
Three-part Mixed

"Two Jests for Fun," by Bill Vollinger
Unison/Two-part

"Turkey in the Straw," by Linda Spevacek
Three-part Mixed; Two-part

"Twelfth-Street Rag," by Linda Spevacek
Three-part Mixed; Two-part

"Um Skit a Rat Trap Si Si Do," by Linda Spevacek
Three-part Mixed; Two-part

"A Whistler's Suite," by Linda Spevacek
Two-part

21 The A to Zs of Teaching

Linda Spevacek

Aim for a higher standard of excellence.

Be the best of who you are.

Confidence comes from knowledge of technique and subjects.

Do your best; forget the rest.

Every student has value.

Find four positive things to say for every correction you make.

Give your best to the world and the best will come back to you.

High-five life every morning!

If it's to be, it's up to me.

Just be yourself.

Keep on smiling.

Love touches the heart; music touches the soul.

Make yourself necessary to someone.

Never let a day go by without humor.

Open your mind—try new techniques, music, styles.

Practice enthusiasm and you will become enthusiastic.

Quiet your mind once a day.

Respect is a two-way street—you get back what you give out.

Start a motivational "quote of the week" in your classroom.

Take time for yourself personally and professionally.

Understand that a bad day is just that…a bad day.

Value your gifts daily.

Winning attitudes must become a habit in your daily teaching.

X out any negative feelings. Start each day with a clean slate.

Youthful thinking will help you avoid burnout.

Zero enthusiasm produces zero results.

APPENDICES

A Appendix A: Publisher Information

Alfred Publishing Company
16320 Roscoe Blvd., Suite 100
P.O. Box 10003
Van Nuys, CA 91410-0003
Phone: (818) 891-5999
Fax: (818) 891-2369
customerservice@alfred.com
www.alfred.com

Alliance Music Publications
4819 Feagan Street
Houston, TX 77007
Phone: (713) 868-9980
Fax: (713) 802-2988
info@alliancemusic.com
www.alliancemusic.com

Boosey & Hawkes, Inc.
35 East 21st Street
New York, NY 10010-6212
Phone: (212) 358-5300
Fax: (212) 358-5303
info@ny.boosey.com
www.boosey.com

BriLee Music Publishing Co.
P.O. Box 210829
Nashville, TN 37221-0829
Phone: (615) 673-6580
Fax: (615) 673-6890
BriLeeMusic@comcast.net
www.brileemusic.com

Carl Fischer, LLC
65 Bleecker Street
New York, NY 10012
Phone: (212) 777-0900
Fax: (212) 477-6996
cf-info@carlfischer.com
www.carlfischer.com

Choristers Guild
2834 W. Kingsley Road
Garland, TX 75041-2498
Phone: (972) 271-1521
Fax: (972) 840-3113
choristers@choristersguild.org
www.choristersguild.org

earthsongs
220 NW 29th Street
Corvallis, OR 97330
Phone: (541) 758-5760
Fax: (541) 754-5887
info@earthsongsmus.com
www.earthsongsmus.com

Hal Leonard Corporation
7777 W. Bluemound Rd.
P.O. Box 13819
Milwaukee, WI 53213
Phone: (414) 774-3630
Fax: (414) 774-3259
halinfo@halleonard.com
www.halleonard.com

Heritage Music Press
A division of The Lorenz Corporation
P.O. Box 802
Dayton, OH 45401-0802
Phone: (937) 228-6118
Fax: (937) 223-2042
copyright@lorenz.com
www.lorenz.com

Hinshaw Music, Inc.
P.O. Box 470
Chapel Hill, NC 27514
Phone: (919) 933-1691
Fax: (919) 967-3399
hinshaw@hinshawmusic.com
www.hinshawmusic.com

Mark Foster
A Division of Shawnee Press, Inc.
Jay Park Plaza
9 Dartmouth Drive Bldg. 4
P.O. Box 1250
Marshalls Creek, PA 18335
Phone: (800) 962-8584
Fax: (800) 345-6842
shawnee-info@shawneepress.com
www.shawneepress.com

Oxford University Press
198 Madison Avenue
New York, NY 10016-4314
Phone: (212) 726-6000
Fax: (212) 726-6444
music@oup-usa.com
www.oup-usa.com

Roger Dean Publishing Co.
A division of The Lorenz Corporation
P.O. Box 802
Dayton, OH 45401-0802
Phone: (937) 228-6118
Fax: (937) 223-2042
copyright@lorenz.com
www.lorenz.com

Santa Barbara Music Publishing
260 Loma Media
Santa Barbara, CA 93103
Phone: (805) 962-5800
Fax: (805) 966-7711
info@sbmp.com
www.sbmp.com

Shawnee Press, Inc.
Jay Park Plaza
9 Dartmouth Drive Bldg. 4
P.O. Box 1250
Marshalls Creek, PA 18335
Phone: (800) 962-8584
Fax: (800) 345-6842
shawnee-info@shawneepress.com
www.shawneepress.com

Walton
A division of Hal Leonard Corporation
7777 W. Bluemound Rd.
P.O. Box 13819
Milwaukee, WI 53213
Phone: (414) 774-3630
Fax: (414) 774-3259
halinfo@halleonard.com
www.halleonard.com

Warner Bros. Publications, Inc.
15800 N.W. 48th Avenue
P.O. Box 4340
Miami, FL 33014
Phone: (305) 620-1500
Fax: (305) 621-4869
wbpsales@warnerchappell.com
www.warnerbrospublications.com

Appendix B: Other Helpful Resources

Body, Mind, Spirit, Voice
A 2002 documentary from the 14th-annual National Choral Conference with Dr. Anton Armstrong and Dr. André Thomas, featuring The American Boychoir
The American Boychoir School, distributed by The Lorenz Corporation (V101)

Building Beautiful Voices
A concise, yet comprehensive study of vocal technique for the choral rehearsal or private instruction
Paul Nesheim with Weston Noble
Roger Dean Publishing Co. (30/1054R)

The Choral Director as Voice Teacher
An instructional video
Linda Spevacek
www.lindaspevacek.com

From the Trenches: Real Insights from Real Choral Educators
Nancy Smirl Jorgensen & Catherine Pfeiler-Bielawski
Heritage Music Press (30/1877H)

In Search of Musical Excellence
Taking Advantage of Varied Learning Styles
Sally Herman
Roger Dean Publishing Co. (30/1022)

Music Survival Kit: Choral Director CD-ROM
A Never-Ending Support System at Your Fingertips
Heritage Music Press (30/1959H)

Sharing Secrets: A Step-by-Step Journey from Unison to Two-part Singing
Karen Bodoin & Phyllis Wolfe White
Heritage Music Press (30/1852H)

Translations and Annotations of Choral Repertoire
Volume I: Sacred Latin Texts
Compiled and Annotated by Ron Jeffers
earthsongs (ISBN: 0-9621532-1-4)

About the Authors

Randy Pagel

Randy Pagel, who received his Bachelor of Music Education from the University of Wisconsin-Oshkosh, and Master of Music from the University of Wisconsin-Madison, teaches at Thurman White Middle School in Henderson, Nevada, where his choirs have performed at state, division and national ACDA and MENC conventions. Randy is a frequent guest conductor and clinician throughout the country, conducting several All-State Honor Choirs and at Orchestra Hall in Chicago and Carnegie Hall in New York City.

He has received numerous awards for teaching, was named University of Wisconsin-Oshkosh "Outstanding Young Alumni," was inducted in the Oshkosh North High School Hall of Fame, and received the Key to the City of Oshkosh. "Randy Pagel Day" was proclaimed in both Henderson, Nevada and Oshkosh, Wisconsin.

Linda Spevacek

With more than 700 published titles, Linda Spevacek has become one of the most successful composers in choral music today. Linda has continued to keep her compositions original and creative while maintaining the consistency and integrity that has given her a world-renowned reputation. Since earning her Bachelors of Arts in Music Education from the University of Wisconsin-Madison, Linda has had extensive involvement with a wide range of choirs and continues to teach seminars for teachers and judge music festivals.

Linda has composed commissions for many groups, including those featured at the national ACDA and MENC conventions. Additionally she was a featured conductor/composer at Carnegie Hall in New York City. Her music has been featured twice on the World's Largest Concert on PBS and performed in the Smetana Hall in Prague, Czechoslovakia at the International Choral Festival. She has won repeated awards from ASCAP and is a member of ASCAP, ACDA, MENC, NATS, and Sigma Alpha Iota. Linda currently resides in Phoenix, Arizona, where she maintains a diverse voice studio in addition to her writing and seminar work.

Personal Reflections from Randy Pagel

My music career got off to an auspicious debut when, at the age of 4, I got lost in a shopping mall and found my way to the toy pianos. I'd never seen a piano before, yet my antics entertained a crowd so large they attracted my mother as she was searching for me. Every year after that, I received a toy piano for Christmas; that is, until it was time for the real thing. My parents, who had no musical background, called Carol Winborne for piano lessons. Ms. Winborne invited me to come in and gave me a few things to practice. The next week, I played a piece that included a teacher's accompaniment, which she played. Without knowing any better, I asked her if *I* could play the "teacher's part." After that, Ms. Winborne informed my parents that I definitely needed *private* lessons, as opposed to the group lessons my parents had contacted her about. I moved ahead with private lessons not knowing how my family could afford them. It wasn't until several years later that I found out Ms. Winborne often gave me lessons free of charge. Upon learning of this kindness, I made up my mind that I would return the favor by always striving to be the best teacher possible.

Every winter, I gathered the neighborhood kids to go Christmas caroling and by the time I was in the seventh grade I was directing our church choir. From then on, I knew I wanted to be a middle school chorus teacher. But I was the class clown, and in detention every day! Then, two things happened that changed my life. First, Mr. Pable, a history teacher and piano tuner and performer—and the detention supervisor—appreciated my musical talent like no other person. With one 5-minute conversation, he convinced me to use my musical and leadership skills to my advantage. Second, as an eighth grader, I was given the role of the Artful Dodger in the high school production of *Oliver!* Because the rehearsals were after school and I had to travel to the high school, I didn't have time to be in detention. I had to behave! I soon understood the power a great teacher has on a student, and the responsibility a musical production can instill.

By the time I was in high school, I participated in all-state choirs and the Dorian Festival in Decorah, Iowa, under the direction of Weston Noble. I was hooked! I also wanted to travel the country as a guest conductor and clinician. To help realize my aspirations, I needed to go to college and pay for music-related expenses. This meant juggling six jobs while in high school: directing the church choir; being a clown (yes, a real clown) at various parties, company picnics and city functions; playing and singing at what felt like every wedding in Oshkosh; working at Ray's Restaurant, a local ma & pa place; serving as a coat checker and bottle boy at the Eagles Club ballroom; and playing piano for Richard's School of the Dance. My experiences at each of these diverse jobs had a major influence on how I teach and work with people.

My undergrad work was at the University of Wisconsin-Oshkosh. There, I studied choral music with Carl Chapman, who often allowed me to work with the choirs and participate in music camps, high school workshops, etc. I studied voice with Frank Hoffmeister, who convinced me to get my masters degree at the University of Wisconsin-Madison. I wanted to begin teaching immediately and wasn't crazy about the idea of putting this dream off, but I had a great deal of trust in Mr. Hoffmeister and followed his advice. It turned out to be the best advice I had ever received from anyone! These teachers demonstrated their skills by stepping back to give opportunities for students to learn, and by giving the best advice possible, even if it's not what the student wants to hear.

During my graduate work at the University of Wisconsin-Madison I was extremely fortunate to work with one of the greatest choral conductors of all time—Robert Fountain. Just being in his presence was enough for me, and I cannot begin to describe everything I learned from him. I studied voice with Mimmi Fulmer, who I continue to correspond with and who continues to have compliments for my students and me.

Upon receiving these degrees, it was off to Las Vegas to embark on my career. Year after year I found my program getting better and better, and under the auspices of Thurman White Middle School principal Frank Lamping we were fortunate enough to perform at many prestigious events. I was also invited to be a guest clinician throughout my home states of Nevada and Wisconsin, but the first "out-of-my-turf" clinic was at the Four Corners Workshop in Flagstaff, Arizona, where Edie Copley is the director. This opportunity was thanks to Kim Barclay-Drusedum, director at Green Valley High School in Henderson, Nevada, into which my middle school feeds. She had all of the attendees use their evaluations to recommend me as the following year's clinician. (When I run for President of the United States, I should put Mrs. Drusedum in charge of the campaign!) The coolest thing about my clinic at the Four Corners Workshop was that I followed Weston Noble, and he stayed for my clinic! Talk about a dream come true!

After many successful years, our choir was invited to the MENC National Convention in Phoenix, Arizona. I definitely wanted to commission a piece, and began to remember how much I loved Linda Spevacek's arrangement of "Shenandoah," which we'd sung when I was in high school. After checking around, I discovered that she was living in the Phoenix area. I called her, and we immediately clicked. Here was this composer who I had admired for many years, and we were now friends! Over the years, we've done several clinics and workshops together, and have gotten to know each other even better. I couldn't believe how much we are alike, including our Wisconsin connections. I will always be indebted to Linda for helping me to solidify my national reputation.

All these experiences led me to the 2003 National ACDA Convention, where I was invited to present three clinics on middle school music. Because taking notes at my workshops is not the easiest thing to do—I talk really, *really* fast—people have often asked if I would write a book. Well, with the persuasion of Linda Spevacek, the confidence of Mary Lynn

Lightfoot and the approval of Geoff Lorenz, this book became a reality.

A great deal of gratitude goes out to my family, friends and colleagues who have been overwhelmingly supportive of my musical endeavors my entire life! I'll never forget how my classmates always asked me to play the piano for them while they listened intently and cheered me on. I still cherish the reception I received upon my return from singing the "National Anthem" at Wrigley Field for the Chicago Cubs, which was broadcast live in every room at Oshkosh North High School.

Finally, a heartfelt thanks goes to the most important teachers we have in our society—our parents. In my case, my parents, Richard and Rosie Pagel, did not teach me much about music, but they taught me the world about being responsible, honest, reliable, and having an endless work ethic.

Randy Pagel

Personal Reflections from Linda Spevacek

When I was growing up, my goal was to be a secretary. I loved to organize and I knew it would be a steady job. The idea that I would have a career in music never entered my mind. No one in my immediate family had ever been to college. We didn't have the money to pay for a college education even if I had wanted to go. But as life unfolded, I experienced many wonders that exceeded even my wildest dreams.

I began playing piano at the age of five. Mom worked odd jobs to make sure I had lessons. In third grade, my music teacher, Miss Sullivan, saw a special talent in me and put me behind the piano accompanying the third- and fourth-grade choir. She gave me pieces in three flats! I practiced so hard as to not be embarrassed in front of my peers. I was further motivated by even the smallest praise I received. Twenty-five years later I sent Miss Sullivan a letter and thanked her for seeing that little light in me. If it weren't for her, I wouldn't have pursued music.

Over the years, I became quite proficient at sightreading, accompanying and performing, as well as singing in a variety of groups. This was, again, due to the insight and guidance of teachers who had honed their craft well, knew how to convey the techniques and also knew how to inspire. The Wisconsin School of Music (the school in Madison where I took lessons) and my piano teacher, Idelle Strelow, saw my potential and helped with scholarships so I could continue piano lessons when, as a high school sophomore, Dad said, "She's good enough." Heck, I could play for church offertory now!

In my senior year of high school I took my first voice lesson. Wow! I didn't know I was a soprano and could hit a high C! In *a cappella* choir I was an alto because I could carry the part and read music. In girls' triple trio I was second soprano for the same reasons. I had developed a register break going into head voice because it was never used! Correcting this break took me years physically, but even longer psychologically. I didn't think I could sing high after all those years doubting that I was a soprano and ignoring my high range.

To get into the University of Wisconsin School of Music I had to get a scholarship. At that time, there was only one full scholarship awarded per year to an entering freshman. I applied, auditioned and to my surprise…won! Again, this is greatly due to the teachers who taught me the techniques that served me well in auditioning. All the theory, exercises and ear training that I fought in high school piano lessons was finally useful!

Over the next four years I had the opportunity to study and learn with more great teachers, many of whose techniques I still use today. John Paton was my college voice teacher and is still a dear friend. He is now well known in the private voice arena, thanks to his many publications and research. I also spent two years in a tough honors theory music program playing Beethoven symphonies and string quartets by score in front of a private audience of yep, you guessed it, the professor wrinkling his nose and peering over his glasses! Central casting could not have picked a better "college professor." (This was the scariest college moment for me, and each of the twelve who were in that class!) In spite of my fear, he taught me so much and without his knowledge and guidance I wouldn't be where I am today. My piano teacher, Carroll Chilton, inspired the drama and passion I have in my teaching to this day. I will be eternally grateful to all those who have inspired me and been great examples of teachers who love their craft, hone their techniques and infuse them into their students and fellow teachers with intensity.

During this time I also began to understand the meaning and depth of a teacher's life. I started to live and breathe it.

Every Saturday I took a Greyhound bus to another town, Sun Prairie, and taught piano lessons and theory classes all day. This was my first real experience teaching and it was so exciting! I was able to begin giving back and yet at the same time I learned so much! I knew then that I had that love for teaching that I'd seen in my own teachers. What a satisfying, rewarding, exciting and yet demanding job!

Finally, I graduated with my degree in music. It was a proud moment for not only me, but for my family. My first real job was as a middle school music teacher in Delavan, Wisconsin. It was a brand new school with lots of money and support, and I could create what I wanted. This position is where I learned to arrange for all combination of voices. I wanted my kids to sound great and there was little music written for their success. I arranged a lot of SSAB for my mixed choir. This created the four-part sound I wanted yet gave the guys a chance to sing together and build confidence. As a public school teacher, I was beginning to give back in yet another way. Plus, there was also an opportunity to direct the high school church choir and adult choir.

After marrying and moving to Idaho, I began to arrange music for my daughter and son's school choirs and work in classrooms as a guest conductor. As fate would have it, Joyce Eilers, a well-known choral composer and teacher, came to our house one evening and heard my children sing one of the arrangements I'd written for their school choir. Joyce told me I should be writing for publication so others could sing my music. In time, with a reminder a year later, I sent Joyce four pieces, all of which were accepted and first printed in The Joyce Eilers Series with Jenson Publications. Joyce was another wonderful mentor who took the time to teach me the ins and outs of both arranging and the publishing business.

Who would have ever known that all these events in my life would combine to produce more than 700 published choral compositions, seven books, thirteen in-service workshops and seminars plus many opportunities to conduct all-state choirs and honor festivals? Who would have ever thought that a shy little girl from Nebraska whose dad was a traveling battery salesman would one day stand on the stage of Carnegie Hall conducting her own music? Who would have ever known? Teachers, that's who.

Music has the power of producing a certain effect on the moral character of the soul, and if it has the power to do this, it's clear that the young must be directed to music and must be educated in it.

—*Aristotle in his* Essay on Politics

How did all of these experiences come together to produce this book? Randy and I have been friends for several years. I first met Randy when he asked me to write a commission for his middle school choir, which was to be premiered at the National MENC Convention in Phoenix. Several years later he asked me to write another commission to be premiered by his select chamber group at the National ACDA Convention in Chicago. It must be said that this group consisted of only 30 middle school singers. However, I knew the high caliber of Randy's work so I wrote an *a cappella* seven-part *divisi* piece that was sung in front of an audience that totaled 7,000 choral directors! His choir performed it with great aplomb!

Since that time, Randy and I have recommended each other for reading sessions, festivals and all-states. And then, last year, at the National ACDA Convention in New York City, Randy presented an interesting session that I attended. Afterward, we were talking about various trials and tribulations of choral directing. We both had so much to share and with such enthusiasm, we could hardly keep up with one another! (If you've never met Randy Pagel or attended one of his sessions you've missed a real treat, not only for the content but also for the excitement and enthusiasm that he exudes! Randy is always on the move, always looking and talking, and always excited about everything!)

Our conversation after this session eventually led to a collective question: "Where can we reach the most teachers?" Randy shared that he'd begun to put some of his ideas down on paper. Then, simultaneously, it hit us—we have great synergy, let's write the book together. Randy motivated me to take this project seriously. With his experience as a conductor, clinician and middle school teacher, and my experience as a voice teacher, composer, conductor and clinician, and the happenstance of our different genders, we felt we would bring a broad, practical perspective to a wide range of topics. Mary Lynn Lightfoot, my editor at Heritage Music Press, happened to be nearby. We shared our conversation with her and her immediate reply was, "Let's do it!"

A trip to Las Vegas (someone has to do it!) and many exchanges, phone conversations and emails later…*voilà*! This process of writing and organizing was truly a joy. We hope you've enjoyed reading and using this material as much as we truly did creating and writing it!

Linda Spevacek